The Six Works of
Dr. Keith A. Buzzell

fifthpress.org

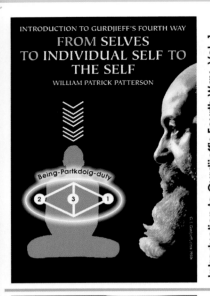

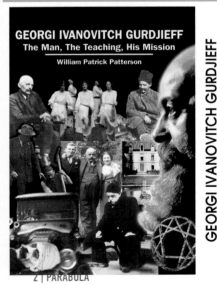
www.GurdjieffLegacy.org

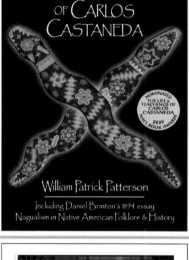
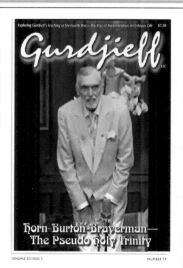
(510) 402-6409

PARABOLA

The Search for Meaning

Mercy & Forgiveness

VOLUME 44 NUMBER 3 FALL 2019

8 His Father Saw Him and Had Compassion *Jesus of Nazareth*
The prodigal son returns

10 A Statement *Martin Scorsese*
The filmmaker writes about forgiveness and acceptance

➤ **11 The Wall and the Mirror** *Kent Jones*
Forgiveness in the work of Martin Scorsese

20 Spiritual Principles in Action *Llewellyn Vaughan-Lee*
The Sufi master on meeting the inner and outer challenges
of our time

26 Forgiving *Mirabai Starr*
The art of mercy

40 A Gesture of Forgiveness *Eleanor O'Hanlon*
Why the whales forgive us

44 Why Forgive? *Richard Smoley*
How to live a freer life

52 In the Name of My Son *Rabbi Tirzah Firestone*
Her son was killed but she chose peace, not vengeance

55 To Forgive *Desmond Tutu*
The Nobel Peace Prize winner explains how to forgive

➤ **56 Painting Enlightenment** *Paula Arai. Artwork by Iwasaki Tsuneo*
A remarkable gallery of Heart Sutra art

64 Mercy *Lee van Laer*
Understanding mercy as a force from on High

➤ *The Good Samaritan* (after Delacroix—detail).
Vincent van Gogh, 1890. Oil on canvas.
Kröller-Müller Museum, Otterlo, Netherlands

➤ **68 Who Decides History's Future?** *Alexandra Haven*
Repairing the damage when cultures collide

74 The Toughest Spiritual Practice *Seane Corn*
A popular yoga teacher ponders forgiving on the mat and off

78 Walking the Path of Forgiveness *Elizabeth Randall*
She befriended a murderer and found release

82 The Power of Forgiveness *Satish Kumar*
A former Jain monk on healing the world

94 Bamboo *Gesshin Claire Greenwood*
How to turn poison into a meal

➤ **102 The Parable of the Prodigal Son** *Pope John Paul II*
The late pontiff on forgiveness, justice, and mercy

EPICYCLES
36 Fujtio
Anonymous / Japanese Noh
Retold by Kenneth E. Lawrence. Artwork by Kumiko Lawrence

90 The Woman Without a Shadow
Anonymous / Scandinavian Folk Talk
Collected by Svend Grundtvig. Retold by Betsy Cornwell

BOOK REVIEW
110 Pray Without Ceasing: The Way of the Invocation in World Religions
Patrick Laude / reviewed by Samuel Bendeck Sotillos

128 ENDPOINT

WHAT IS A PARABOLA?

A parabola is one of the most elegant
forms in nature. It is the arc of a thrown
ball and the curve of a cast fishing line and
the arch of a suspension bridge. A
parabola is also the arc of a spiritual
quest—seekers leave the known for the
unknown, coming home again transformed by a new understanding.

Parabolas have an unusual and crucial
property: as in a parabola-shaped satellite
dish, all the beams of energy that strike a
parabola's face converge at a single point.
This point is called the focus. Each issue
of *PARABOLA* has its own focus: one of
the timeless themes or questions of
human existence.

TO SUBSCRIBE or update subscription: Call 1–877–593–2521 or send request to PARABOLA, P.O. Box 3000, Denville, NJ
07834. Please allow six weeks for change of address. For fastest service, visit www.PARABOLA.org.

PARABOLA (ISSN: 0362–1596), 20 West 20th Street,
2nd floor, New York, NY 10011, is published quarterly
by the Society for the Study of Myth and Tradition,
Inc., a not-for-profit organization. Contributions are
tax-deductible to the full extent of applicable law. To
donate, or for other questions call 212-822-8806.

SUBSCRIPTION RATES Print only (US): $39.95 yearly,
$69.95 for two years, $89.95 for three years. Digital
only: one year $29.95 to any location.

POSTMASTER Send address changes to
PARABOLA. P.O. Box 3000, Denville, NJ 07834.
Periodicals postage paid at New York, NY
and additional mailing offices.

EDITORIAL & ADVERTISING PARABOLA. 20 West 20th
Street, 2nd floor, New York, NY 10011. Editorial
phone/email: 212-822-8806; editorial@parabola.org;
advertising phone/email: 510-548-1680;
parabola@gpr4ads.com. lease include SASE if mail
response is required.

WEBSITE www.parabola.org

DISTRIBUTION For U.S. & Canada: Curtis Circulation
Company: 856.910.2088. www.curtiscirc.com.
Other foreign distribution: Daimon Verlag,
+(41)(55) 412 22 66 www.daimon.ch

MICROFORM COPIES are available from University
Microfilms, Inc. PARABOLA is indexed in the *Religion
Index of Periodicals, Abstracts of English Studies,
Book Review Index, Current Comments, Human-
ities Index, Humanities Abstracts, Humanities
International Complete, CERDIC, Religion and
Theological Abstracts,* and InfoTrac's *Expanded
Academic Index.*

VOLUME 44, NO. 3, FALL 2019

Two acclaimed filmmakers open this issue of *Parabola*: Martin Scorsese, director of TAXI DRIVER, RAGING BULL, CASINO, KUNDUN, SILENCE, and other masterpieces including this Fall's offering, THE IRISHMAN; and Kent Jones, creator of this year's DIANE and director of the New York Film Festival. Scorsese writes of forgiveness; Jones discusses how forgiveness informs and illuminates Scorsese's movies.

What stands out in both men's essays and in their art is an understanding that we each exist in a web of meaningful relationship; that what we do matters, that we each have a responsibility to others and to the world. This critical point is explored further in the issue's next essay, by Sufi master Llewellyn Vaughan-Lee, who details his evolution toward spiritual activism.

That activism—taking responsible action toward a noble aim—finds no more fertile ground than in the practice of mercy and forgiveness. "Forgive us our debts," Jesus taught, "as we forgive our debtors." He also taught that the Kingdom of God is within; and so it follows that we should practice mercy and forgiveness not only toward others but toward ourselves as well. As Nobel Peace Prize winner Desmond Tutu points out in this issue, failure to forgive "locks you in a state of victimhood," and when you forgive "you are no longer chained to the perpetrator."

These ideas are explored throughout the issue in entries ranging from Mirabai Starr on the art of mercy to Seane Corn on forgiving the unforgiveable; from a meditation on why whales forgive us their slaughter to the story of an Israeli woman forsaking vengeance for her son's murder; from a consideration by Pope John Paul II of the Parable of the Prodigal Son to a remarkable gallery of paintings celebrating the merciful Heart Sutra, and much more.

May this Fall 2019 issue of *Parabola* benefit us all in our search for peace and understanding, for mercy and forgiveness.

—Jeff Zaleski

"**AND HE AROSE** and came to his father. But when he was still a great way off, his father saw him and had compassion, and ran and fell on his neck and kissed him. And the son said to him, 'Father, I have sinned against heaven and in your sight, and am no longer worthy to be called your son.'

"But the father said to his servants, 'Bring out the best robe and put it on him, and put a ring on his hand and sandals on his feet. And bring the fatted calf here and kill it, and let us eat and be merry; for this my son was dead and is alive again; he was lost and is found.'"

Luke 15:20-24 New King James Version

The Return of the Prodigal Son (detail). Rembrandt Harmenszoon van Rijn, 1669. Oil on canvas. The Hermitage, St. Petersburg

A Statement from Martin Scorsese

I've subscribed to *Parabola* for thirty years, and I've saved every copy of the magazine. I always look forward to reading the latest issue. It's given me spiritual sustenance—no other way to say it.

The theme of this issue is Forgiveness, and that's a perfect response to a moment in time when unforgiving words and actions are not just celebrated but sold as courage.

It takes real courage to forgive, because it means discarding your anger and indignation, always readily available and therefore dependable, and hacking out a piece of common ground.

Forgiveness of your enemies…forgiveness of your friends and loved ones… and then forgiving yourself: an entirely different kind of question.

To find the courage and the patience and the understanding to see, and from there to accept, is a lifelong practice.

Parabola has guided and provoked and comforted me along my way.

Martin Scorsese. Martin Scorsese Collection, NY

Martin Scorsese (l.) and Robert De Niro (r.) in *Taxi Driver*. Martin Scorsese Collection, NY

The Wall and the Mirror: Forgiveness in the Work of Martin Scorsese

Kent Jones

"If I were God, I'd forgive the whole world."
Robert Bresson, L'ARGENT

THREE YEARS AGO, just before I started shooting my first fiction film, I found myself reading and re-reading a collection of essays by Flannery O'Connor, a writer I hadn't returned to since I was in my twenties. In that collection is an essay called "Catholic Novelists and Their Readers," assembled after her death from drafts of a lecture she delivered on the titular subject. O'Connor deals with the question of fiction written for and marketed to "typical" mid-century American Roman Catholic readers. On *The Foundling*, written by none other than Cardinal Spellman himself, she is merciless. "You do have the satisfaction of knowing that if you buy a copy of *The Foundling*," she writes, "what you are helping are the orphans to whom the proceeds go; and afterwards you can always use the book as a doorstop." As for the many less innocuous "Catholic novels" then on the market, she makes even shorter shrift: "…these are novels that, by the author's efforts to be edifying, leave out half or three-fourths of the facts of human existence and are therefore not true to the mysteries we know by faith or those we perceive simply by observation."

It was the following passage, though, that really struck me. "St. Thomas Aquinas says that art does not require rectitude of the appetite, that it is wholly concerned with the good of that which is made. He says that a work of art is a good in itself, and this is a truth that the modern world has largely forgotten. We are not content to stay within our limitations and make something that is simply a good in and by itself. Now we want to make something that will have some utilitarian value. Yet what is good in itself glorifies God because it reflects God. The artist has his hands full and does his duty if he attends to his art. He can safely leave evangelizing to the evangelists. He must first of all be aware of his limitations as an artist—for art transcends its limitations only by staying within them."

I read these words for the first time in a quiet empty chapel at the east end of the Cathedral of St. John the Divine. Then I did two things that I often do: I transcribed them in my notebook, and I shared them with Martin Scorsese. Who had, as it turns out, been reading O'Connor's letters at the same time.

Marty and I have known each other for almost three decades, and I wasn't at all surprised that he was reading O'Connor. I didn't wonder if he would find the quoted passage interesting. I knew he would, because he *lives* those words.

In 1977, the great French director Robert Bresson was interviewed by Paul Schrader for *Film Comment* magazine on the occasion of his most recent film, *The Devil Probably.* "The young man in my film is looking for something on top of life, but he doesn't find it. He goes to church to seek it, and he doesn't find it. At night he goes to Notre Dame, to find God, alone. He says lines like this, 'When you come in a church, or in a cathedral, God is there'—it is the line of his death—'but if a priest happens to come, God is not there anymore.' This is why, although I am very religious—was very religious, more or less—I can't go to church in the last four or five years when these people are making their new mass. It is not possible." Bresson's film ends with his spiritually bereft hero committing suicide—a mortal sin. At the time of

*To become attuned to art is to become attuned to
the pure sensation of being alive, because
you are seeing it embodied in all its mystery.*

the interview, Schrader (raised in the Calvinist Christian Reformed Church) had just shot his own first feature and before that had written TAXI DRIVER, which is indebted to Bresson's PICKPOCKET and DIARY OF A COUNTRY PRIEST and which ends with a mass murder committed in the name of a grand delusion of divine rectitude.

I was a teenager when TAXI DRIVER came out, and I saw it somewhere in the neighborhood of fifteen or sixteen times in the local theater and then at the drive-in. The topic of bloodshed on the big screen was red hot in those days, and one got used to hearing and reading that movies like TAXI DRIVER were having a "negative influence" on the culture. To experience the actual film, as opposed to the Cultural Conversation piece, had nothing to do with frozen "concepts" or "ideas," the trafficking of which has increased a thousandfold in the forty-plus years since. Of course, there were films that did nothing *but* traffic in the latest "issues" and "ideas," and there are many more of them now—they are, in fact, not so much films as arrays of "culturally resonant" touchpoints illustrated with moving images that are then assembled in beguiling and occasionally scintillating patterns. Some of them win multiple awards.

TAXI DRIVER, on the other hand, like MEAN STREETS or RAGING BULL or CASINO or SILENCE or THE IRISHMAN, is made, in the sense that O'Connor defined. Like any real work of art, it traffics in nothing but its own immediate materials and touches on matters of cultural concern only incidentally and as a consequence of deep engagement with the shared

Willem Dafoe (l.) and Martin Scorsese (r.), *The Last Temptation of Christ.* Martin Scorsese Collection, NY

ongoing world. One can take a stab at naming and elucidating its themes, but such descriptions will always remain provisional, simply because the film is true only to itself. It grows organically from a felt sense of life. This is what William Carlos Williams meant when he wrote that the aim of any artist should be not to copy nature but to imitate it. To copy is to remain safe in the realm of appearances. To imitate the processes of nature is to act, and to delve into the heart of our mystery.

For that reason, there can be no such thing as a great Catholic film or a great Calvinist film or a great Buddhist film. To set out on such an undertaking is inimical to the work of the artist. "We Catholics are very much given to the Instant Answer," wrote O'Connor, and the same could be said of many organized religions and spiritual practices. "Fiction doesn't have any. It leaves us, like Job, with a renewed sense of mystery."

As it was for O'Connor, Marty's need to see, to make, to transmit was intensified and purified by illness—in Marty's case, asthma. "I was allergic to everything around me, including animals, trees, grass—everything," he told me during a conversation that we recorded for another purpose a few years back. "I could not go to the country. They would always have to take me back that night or the next day. The humidity… and the *pollen*… But what it was, was that it separated you from everybody. And it made you aware of an adult world in a way that was…quite unique. You spent a lot more time with the rhythm of that life, with the concerns of the adults—you were privy to all the discussions, what's right and what's wrong, whose obligation this is or that is. And it just made you more *aware*— aware of how the people were feeling, what the body language around you was, aware of your own *sensitivity.*

"And I thought: that's the key. Even if we might feel that it's a punishing God, a torturing God, we have to remember that we're the ones doing the torturing, so we're the ones we have to be merciful with."

You became sharpened, I think. Yet, in making a film, you can be extremely *insensitive*, too. But within that determination that you need to actually *make* a film, you incorporate that sensitivity." Determination, sensitivity, and solitude.

I remember sitting in the living room as a child with my parents, transfixed by a movie showing on television. My parents watched and they also went on talking, asking if this or that actress was alive or dead, what was the weather supposed to be like tomorrow, and "could you go to the kitchen and get me a Fresca?" Marty had the same experience. "For everybody else, it's just another 'movie,' and meanwhile, for you…it's life and death up there."

That's the great paradox. To *know* what you love, to *know* what you want to extend and transmit to the world because something has been transmitted to *you* through art and created a spark, is to know loneliness and real solitude, because no one else can share it. But it is also to know the deepest love for those around you and the world they've created. To become attuned to art is to become attuned to the pure sensation of being alive, because you are seeing it embodied in all its mystery.

Marty was drawn to cinema and to the church, simultaneously. "The profound impression of Catholicism at a very early age is something that I've always related *back* to," he said. "One

may read or become interested in many different ways…I'm interested in how people perceive God, or perceive the world of the intangible—all people, everywhere. But *my* way has always been through Catholicism." Within the world of Little Italy in the 1950s, many of the elements that are constants in Christian sermonizing were immediately and tangibly present. The "least among us" lived in the shadows of the Third Avenue El and in the bars and missions and flophouses on the old Bowery. The "criminal element," as it was called, cast a different kind of shadow over the neighborhood, and violence and tenderness and beauty existed in very close proximity. The priests at Old St. Patrick's Cathedral dealt with the world around them, now long gone, as it *was*. "I was very aware as a child of a God of storms and lightning and punishment, and then it was balanced by these priests, who showed me another side of it. Their words were one thing, but their actions were something else entirely. They were street priests— Diocesan priests. They didn't force you to do things. They *cajoled*. They may have been very strong in their language with you at times, and they would lecture you about the wages of sin and impure thoughts and so on, but there was an extraordinary love. It was an amazing experience."

The priest that had the most profound effect on Marty was Father

Sharon Stone (l.) and Robert De Niro (r.) in *Casino*. Martin Scorsese Collection, NY

Principe, who passed away last year in his nineties. He can be seen in the PBS documentary MARTIN SCORSESE DIRECTS, made around the time of GOODFELLAS. His presence is as straight and swift as an arrow. "I wanted to follow in Father Principe's footsteps, so to speak, and I went to a preparatory seminary but I failed out the first year. Because I realized at age fifteen that a vocation is something very special, and it can't be because you want to be like somebody else: you have to have a true calling."

There could also be a calling to do something else, namely cinema, and of that Marty has spoken for many years and under a variety of circumstances with great eloquence. Those are words of inspiration, but they are also words of caution to anyone who imagines going into a "career" in filmmaking the way one would go into a career in law or business. It is possible, he is careful to remember, to become a "professional" director. To be a filmmaker is something else again.

I n the mid-1960s, just as Marty was starting to make his own first feature, the country was flying apart at the seams and he began to question his own relationship to Catholicism. "I was changing and I didn't *know* if I was going to become mature in the religion. Vietnam was declared a holy war, and there was a great deal of confusion and doubt and sadness for the whole country, and for me. So seeing Bresson's film version of *DIARY OF A COUNTRY PRIEST* at that time gave me hope. The characters in that film are really suffering, and they're being punished, by others and by themselves, throughout. And at one point, the priest says to a woman in his parish, 'God is not a torturer—He just wants us to be merciful with ourselves.' And I thought: *that's* the key. Even if we might *feel* that it's a punishing God, a torturing God, we have to remember that *we're* the ones doing the torturing, so *we're* the ones we have to be merciful with."

It's impossible to singularize the work of an artist, to summarize his or her preoccupations. However, I think that it's just to look at Marty's work through the lens of mercy. He has made many films about people who torture themselves with delusions—delusions of cheap grandeur, as in *Casino* and *The Wolf of Wall Street*; delusions of ease and comfort and misplaced certainty, as in *GoodFellas* and *The Age of Innocence*; spiritual delusions, as in *Mean Streets* and *The Last Temptation of Christ* and *Silence*. These delusions are intensified versions of the same delusions from which we've all suffered. The manner and pace of human change in those films is properly aligned with lived life, which is precisely why these characters who commit the worst imaginable actions radiate humanity: for them, mercy is either out of reach or unthinkable, but it is always *present*, even as a felt absence. The characters in these films believe that they *can not* be kind to themselves or to each other because they are in the thrall of grand dreams and even

grander misunderstandings of rectitude, fairness, and retribution carried over from some earlier moment in their lives. The majestic unspoolings of excess (in *GoodFellas* and *Casino*) and extravagance and ceremony (in *The Age of Innocence*) and wild flights of craziness and cruelty and group euphoria and violence (in *Mean Streets* and *Taxi Driver* and *Raging Bull*) resonate so deeply because they're framed within impermanence and instability—the characters fail to recognize their circumstances but *we* feel them in the rhythm of the storytelling, in the sudden yet tender seizing on small homely details (like the cuts to the coffee cups in *Raging Bull* or the stray faces in *Mean Streets*, or the move into the garish Christmas tree ornament in *GoodFellas*) that will soon be lost forever. Somehow, they carry and transmit a possibility: forgiveness and redemption are always just around the corner. This is what gives the movies their throat-catching poignancy.

Right before Marty and Robert De Niro were set to start production on

Harvey Keitel in *Mean Streets*. Martin Scorsese Collection, NY

"After everything that's happened in history, after all the ways the world has changed and been overwhelmed by thought, political and economic theories, different systems of governing, different systems of belief...it always comes down to the person in the room with you."

RAGING BULL, they had a meeting with the new executives at United Artists. One of the execs asked them why they wanted to make a movie about Jake La Motta. "The guy's a cockroach," he said. De Niro's response was simple: "No, he's not." RAGING BULL poses a question to its audience: how can someone who cannot articulate the terms of his own humanity find his way to it? The answer is in his own being, his very presence, and in the presence of the world around him. The answer is in those coffee cups, and in his brother gently tucking his hair under his hood before he walks to the championship bout, and in the laying of hands he observes so suspiciously between his brother and his wife and the mob boss who comes to visit as he prowls his Detroit hotel suite in a black polo shirt that electrifies the screen.

I was twenty years old when RAGING BULL came out. I skipped school to see it with my best friend on the day it opened in New York. I was stunned and so was he. And perhaps a little puzzled at first, because I'd never seen anything like it. I still haven't. And I took in the film on a physical level, which is as it should be. When Jake La Motta finds his way to forgiveness, he literally comes up against a brick wall, in a Miami jail cell. Out of anger at his jailers and anger at himself—in the end, one and the same—he tries to beat his way through the

walls, with his fists, his forearms, his head, until he finally comes to a stop and is able to say the simple words: "I'm not that bad."

"In RAGING BULL, he's the one who has to stop punishing himself," Marty told me. "Yes, he's punishing everyone else around him at the same time, but he has to start with himself. And at the end, when he looks in the mirror, he's found a way to start finding some mercy for himself. You gotta *face* yourself. The problem is actually *forgiving* yourself. It's hard. Many people can't even imagine it. And...maybe the word 'forgiving' is pompous...*accepting* yourself is what it is. *Living with* yourself. Because that might make it easier to live with other people, and be good to other people."

As Thelma Schoonmaker, who edited RAGING BULL and every one of Marty's narrative films since, once put it to me, "RAGING BULL isn't a movie, it's a poem." It's a poem of mercy, the road to which is paved with horrible violence, jealousy, paranoia, loss, but also fleeting beauty and abiding love. And it could only have been composed by artists with a fierce and binding commitment to the least among us...and within us. "The practicing is not in a building where you meet at a certain time on a certain day of the week to perform certain rituals," observed Marty, in an echo of Charlie's first words in MEAN STREETS (spoken in

Robert De Niro (l.) and Martin Scorsese (r.), *Raging Bull.* Martin Scorsese Collection, NY

voiceover by the director himself). "The practicing is outside, and it's really *everything* you do, good or bad. And that's been the struggle. It's in your actions, and how you relate to the people around you. It's not necessarily a matter of the good that you create, because you might think that you're doing what is good for others when actually you're *not*. Maybe you're just placating your own conscience, you know? There's also the damage one does. So the way that religion and spirituality play out is in your behavior with others. After everything that's happened in history, after *all* the ways the world has changed and been overwhelmed by thought, political and economic theories, different systems of governing, different systems of belief…it always comes down to the person in the room with you. That's really what it is. And whether

you're successful at it or not, it's in the *trying*. It really comes down to that. And this has been, for me, over the years, very difficult because of my absorption in work. Because I express it in film."

We all pray that the people around us will be able to forgive themselves. We diagnose the struggles of others so easily, and we are shocked when they see and name *our* struggles. To forgive, or to accept, is to *see*—everyone and everything, including ourselves. One must *work* to see. And one begins the work by learning to recognize the difference between that which momentarily intrigues, or that which promises much and delivers little, and that which actually illuminates. This is what I recognized in MEAN STREETS when I saw it for the first time, forty-six years ago, and in so many films and loving gestures since. ◆

Spiritual Principles in Action: A Story for a Younger Generation

Llewellyn Vaughan-Lee

A Sufi master on taking responsibility for our world

Glastonbury Festival, England, 1971. Photograph by Paul Townsend

*In answer to a question from a thirty-one-year-old person,
"What advice do you have for people my age in dealing
with a world that tells us we are nothing but material
mechanisms, and has almost no concept of the soul?"*

*Through meditation and prayer,
going deep within, we find something
beyond the illusions of the outer world—
we dip into love's infinite ocean.*

CHAPTER ONE

I GREW UP IN AN ENGLAND still dreary in the post-war years. It was a grey world aspiring to middle-class materialism—a TV, a washing machine, even a car! Then in the mid to late sixties, another color entered the spectrum of consciousness. The Beatles went to India to meditate with the Maharishi, and orange-robed Hare Krishna devotees could be seen dancing and chanting on Oxford Street in London. Spirituality in all of its flavors and colors began to arrive in the West.

This awakening was part of my adolescence. When I was sixteen I began to practice Zen meditation, and I experienced an inner dimension of emptiness completely different from the world of my schoolboy classrooms. When I was eighteen I practiced hatha yoga (until I damaged my right knee from sitting too long in the lotus position) and became macrobiotic, learning to bake my own unleavened bread. I studied sacred geometry and built geodesic domes. I attended one of the first Glastonbury Festivals, where the pyramid stage was supposed to transmit spiritual vibrations. Then, when I was nineteen, I met my spiritual teacher, a white-haired Russian lady who had just come back from India, where she had been trained as a Sufi master. My heart became awakened to a love I

never knew existed. Many friends at the time followed similar paths—exploring Buddhist meditation in the monasteries of South East Asia, reading Tibetan texts, chanting Hindu mantras, or whirling with Sufi dervishes. We felt that we were part of a spiritual movement that was going to change the world. Something was alive in a new way; a new spark of consciousness was present.

Looking back over almost half a century, I can see how our journey, the story of my generation, was to help bring these practices and teachings to the West, to help something come alive in our materialistic Western consciousness. Meditation groups formed, ashrams were built, and many of us practiced ways to access different states of consciousness. We were naïve and optimistic, expecting this infusion of spiritual consciousness to change the world. Sadly, or more realistically, while it changed our world, the world around us only became more enamored of materialism, technology, and the "toys of triviality." And, as the Seventies moved into the Eighties and then the Nineties, many of the gurus became corrupted, mainly by sex or money, and many sincere seekers disillusioned. The innocence of those early years faded into the harsher light of daily life.

But something remained. There was a shift in consciousness—this new color in the spectrum remained—along with the various spiritual practices and texts that had come from the East. Those of us who remained true to our practice, who lived our meditation and spiritual values, held this shift in consciousness, and integrated it into our daily life. We listened to our dreams and our hearts, we opened to inner experiences beyond the physical. We lived the story of our soul.

Then, at the beginning of the twenty-first century, something within me shifted, and I was shown how spiritual values belong not just to the inner journey of the individual, but have a vital part to play in the outer world. Traditionally the seeker turns away from the outer towards the inner, seeking the truth that, for example, in Sufism can only be found within the heart. Through meditation and prayer, going deep within, we find something beyond the illusions of the outer world—we dip into love's infinite ocean. We experience the reality of the Self and the oneness that belongs to all that exists— what the Sufis call "unity of being," and for the Buddhist is experienced as Buddha nature with its awareness of the interdependence of existence ("dependent co-arising"). But I began to realize that this "consciousness of oneness" was needed in our outer world, that our world was suffering from a misguided consciousness of separation, which is the consciousness of the rational self and ego: we are separate from the Earth and separate from each other.

This focus on awakening to oneness gradually evolved into my Spiritual Ecology work of recent years, giving a spiritual perspective to our present ecological crisis. When I began this work over a decade ago, "oneness" was still a fringe "spiritual" idea. Spirituality and ecology were rarely associated. Environmentalists thought spiritual practitioners were "new age" and not activist enough, while apart from a few "engaged Buddhists" and others, spiritual practices and teachings were focused on self-development and the individual inner journey. But I am very happy that in the last few years, oneness, interconnectivity, or what the Buddhist monk Thich Nhat Hanh calls "interbeing," has become much more part of the mainstream, and central to understanding the ecological crisis—that we need to respond from an awareness of the Earth as a living organic whole.

As Pope Francis expressed so beautifully in his encyclical ON CARE FOR OUR COMMON HOME, we need to listen to "the cry of the earth and the cry of the poor." We can no longer afford to live in a way of exploitation and division. We need to take full responsibility for our world and work together to return to a balanced and sustainable way of life for humanity and all of creation—to care for both the soil and the soul.

CHAPTER TWO

As I have mentioned, condensed into these paragraphs is almost half a century's journey of living, and also holding, a quality of consciousness radically different to that of the environment I was born into. In its broadest terms this consciousness is *the awareness of a spiritual reality whose values are very different to the ego-driven material focus of our present civilization.*

Sadly the materialistic values of the Fifties have now morphed into a global monster, exploiting and ravaging the Earth in a way that can only result in mutual self-destruction. Still, while there are those continuing this nightmare of "business as usual"—the global corporations and politicians who pursue only economic growth or greed—there are others who have real "care for our common home," who hear the cry of the Earth and the pressing need to live from a place of unity. Maybe we have already passed the "tipping point" of unforeseen ecological consequences: temperatures rising, rivers and oceans polluted, and air made toxic. But spiritual consciousness still has a vital role to play as our world spins out of balance.

The next chapter of this story of spirituality must bring these values, this quality of consciousness, into action to help heal and restore our dying world.

Yet I believe it is no longer enough just to hold this awareness—*we have to bring it into action*. Many people who read my book SPIRITUAL ECOLOGY: THE CRY OF THE EARTH responded, "What should I do?" The next chapter of this story of spirituality must bring these values, this quality of consciousness, into action to help heal and restore our dying world. I firmly believe that this is the calling for the next generation, for those who have the energy and passion to act from a place of service and love for the Earth—and, especially important, from a place of unity. (SPIRITUAL ECOLOGY: THE CRY OF THE EARTH is a collection of essays by spiritual teachers, scientists, and others, that proposes the need for a spiritual response to our present environmental crisis.)

This is the challenge facing those of the millennial generation who sense that life is something more than the accumulation of "stuff," who have heard the cry of the Earth, which is also the cry of their own soul. How can we help the world in this time of transition? How can we participate creatively in our lives and our communities? There is much work to be done, a work founded upon the principles of oneness and unity, a work that recognizes that all of life is sacred and whole. Life is calling to us and it desperately needs our attention; around us are what Thich Nhat Hanh calls "bells of mindfulness," which we need to hear and then respond to—hear with our hearts and respond with our hands.

There are many ways to participate, to work towards ecological wholeness, from forming a community of urban gardeners, to developing new economic models based on generosity and sharing rather than acquisition, such as "pay it forward." It is for each person to find the community and initiative that speaks most to their nature, their unique offering. And central to this work is that we are here to help each other. And I firmly believe that—while some global initiatives are vital, like reducing carbon emissions—most initiatives should be small groups of people coming together in different ways. Governments and politicians are too bound to the idea of continued

People's Climate March, New York City, 2014. Photograph by by the *South Bend Voice*

"economic growth" to commit to real change. Instead the world needs to be regenerated in an organic, cellular way, the way life recreates itself.

I also believe that it is important for anyone committing to this work to develop their own spiritual practice—especially helpful is a meditation practice that is done every day. It can be a mindfulness meditation, watching the breath, the Christian practice of centering prayer, or a Sufi heart meditation. It could also be walking in a sacred manner, being aware of our connection to the sacred Earth with every step we take. What matters is that our practice connects us to what is most deep and enduring within us, a Source beyond the illusions of the ego and the many distractions of the outer world. This practice can support and protect us, and inwardly guide us in our work.

And if I have learned anything from my journey, I've learned what matters most is love. Love is the most powerful force in creation, and it is our love for the Earth that will heal what we have desecrated, that will guide us through this wasteland and help us to bring light back into our darkening world. As in the words of the poet Wendell Berry, "The world...can be redeemed only by love." Love links us all together in the most mysterious ways, and love can guide our hearts and hands. And the central note of love is oneness. Love speaks the language of oneness, of unity rather than separation. ◆

Reprinted here from Llewellyn Vaughn-Lee's essay "Spiritual Principles in Action" from *JOURNEYS AND AWAKENINGS: WISDOM FOR SPIRITUAL TRAVELERS* (2019) edited by Robert Corman and others, by kind permission of Sacred Spirit Books, an imprint of Monkfish Book Publishing Company, Rhinebeck, New York

Guanyin in the Tidal Sound cave at Mt Potal. Anonymous, Qing Dynasty. National Palace Museum, Taipei, Taiwan

Celebrating the many ways of mercy

Forgiving: The Art Of Mercy

Mirabai Starr

I'M SORRY. I'm so sorry that I broke your heart, that I was too demanding of your approval, that I forgot to put your name in my acknowledgments. I'm sorry I ignored you at the poetry reading and didn't bother to correct the perception that I don't care about you. I'm sorry I didn't attend your concert, your wedding, your funeral. I'm sorry I talked too much at the dinner party. I'm sorry I was so quiet. I'm sorry I gave you a low grade on your midterm exam. I'm sorry I was a mother who put my relationships with men ahead of my children. I'm sorry I was the kind of mother who hovered like a blimp and smothered you. I'm sorry I interpreted your rejection as rejection, rather than as the cry for love that it really was.

I forgive you. I forgive you for dying young. I forgive you for drinking too much and acting like an asshole. I forgive you for talking about me behind my back. I forgive you for running over my neighbor and her daughter who were out for a walk. I forgive you for leaving your girlfriend when she told you she was pregnant. I forgive you for accusing me of being arrogant when I was just excited. I forgive you for not seeing me.

I forgive you for being blind to your own shadow, for your participation in institutionalized racism, misogyny, heteronormativity. I forgive you for your anti-Semitic jokes and your Islamophobic remarks. I forgive you for lobbying for ownership of assault weapons, amassing a nuclear arsenal, building a wall to keep out people of color and separate children from their parents. I forgive you for genocide against the indigenous peoples of this and every other continent. I forgive you for the Holocaust that exterminated my ancestors like bugs. I forgive you for the slave trade, for sex trafficking, for treating garbage collectors like garbage. I forgive you for putting profits ahead of people, technology ahead of clean air and water, head ahead of heart.

Forgiving you was the best thing I ever did. Forgiving you set the bird of my heart winging through the universe.

Every wisdom tradition on the planet emphasizes that compassion is the quintessence of the holy.

QUAN YIN

She is the bodhisattva of compassion, the embodiment of loving-kindness, the personification of mercy. She Who Hears the Cries of the World; She Who Sees the Wounds of the World. She is the incarnation of the Buddha of compassion, who had the option of merging into the boundless ocean of Nirvana and chose instead to return to the wheel of samsara (births, deaths, rebirths) in feminine form, as Quan Yin, to comfort and awaken all beings until every being is free from suffering.

Eleven-faced Kannon. Wood, ninth century. Domyoji Temple, Fujiidera, Japan. Photograph by Ogawa Seiyou

It is said that Quan Yin was born a woman, Miao Shan, and that, like so many legendary female saints, she flowered in the face of persecution. Her parents wanted a boy child, and they did their best to get rid of Miao Shan as soon as possible. In the meantime, they put her to work doing the most arduous household tasks. Not only did her labors fail to bring Miao Shan down, but she drew the attention of the forest creatures, who joined forces to help

her. The mice threaded her needles, the rabbits swept the courtyard, the deer split kindling for the cook fire.

When it came time for her to be married off, Miao Shan informed her parents that she preferred to become a nun. They refused. She insisted. Finally her father sent her to a convent of his own choosing, but only after striking a deal with the abbess that Miao Shan be assigned the grungiest duties so she would be discouraged from monastic life.

Miao Shan was appointed to the convent hospice, where she was meant to tend infectious wounds, clean up all manner of bodily fluids, and prepare corpses for burial. This job, of course, was perfect for Miao Shan. She not only cared for her patients' physical needs, but also loved them through their deepest suffering. She sang to them and sat with them in silence. And when they died, she accompanied them to the otherworld to make sure they were safe.

When her father found out that Miao Shan was thriving where he hoped she would capitulate, he ordered her execution. As the henchman raised his ax over her head, Miao Shan looked into his eyes and forgave him for what he was about to do. She assured him that he would not bear the karmic burden for this deed. Unable to carry out an act of violence upon such an angelic being, he threw down his ax, which shattered into a thousand pieces. Miao Shan was swept up in a pearly mist and transported to a nearby island, where she spent the rest of her life in meditation. When she died, she became Quan Yin, embodiment of selfless service and sweet mercy.

Do not be fooled. Miao Shan's humility was not compliant; it was subversive! Quan Yin's compassion is not indulgent; it is subversive! It invites us to lay down our weapons and open our hearts. The tender attributes of the feminine do not render her weak and ineffectual. They glorify her. Our vulnerability is our strength. Our capacity to forgive is our superpower.

MAKING AMENDS

Every wisdom tradition on the planet emphasizes that compassion is the quintessence of the holy. The Arabic word *rahim*, found in the opening lines of the Qur'an and repeated many times a day in the *salat* (daily prayers), means "compassion." Rahim is also the word for "womb." Forgiveness is the very face of the Divine Feminine. Each time we allow mercy to enter the shattered spaces of our hearts, we participate in the divine nature. To forgive ourselves is to forge a contract with the Divine Mother: I will mirror you in my own soul. Yet this is not so much a decision as an allowing. It is grace.

Women have a tendency to overapologize. Not all women, of course. But many of us have been conditioned to avoid taking up space in this world, expressing our opinions, asking for what we want. We are compelled to beg forgiveness for being and may use this compulsion as a kind of preemptive technique, accusing ourselves before we can be accused and thereby escaping condemnation. While we may find this habit of apologizing for every little thing annoying in others, it's harder to catch our own self-deprecating behaviors. We would never speak to a beloved child the way we talk to ourselves sometimes in the middle of the night when we can't help rewinding the tape of our lives and blaming ourselves for a thousand missteps. We wouldn't even treat a stranger so harshly. What would happen if we cultivated tenderness toward our own broken being? What revolution would unfold if we embraced the teachings of the mystics and practiced cherishing ourselves?

Of course, making amends is almost always a vital spiritual practice. Every tradition has rituals for taking a moral inventory, asking for and receiving forgiveness. They all encourage us to engage in concrete action to rectify any damage caused by our shortcomings while acknowledging that we are likely to mess up again and offering techniques for growing our consciousness around the kinds of behaviors that caused us to miss the mark. The vulnerability such practices engender is in itself holy ground. We soften our grip on the separate self and leave the ego undefended, affirming our interdependence with all beings and finding our footing in the human condition.

TREASURE YOURSELF

My friend Ondrea Levine is a prophet of self-forgiveness. Beloved partner of the late Stephen Levine, revered for his pioneering work with conscious dying, Ondrea is a powerful teacher in her own right. Her teaching is deceptively simple and cuts like a diamond through our calcified self-hatred: *Treasure yourself.*

There is often a sense of peace that descends on our hearts when we cultivate the courage to forgive. We are tangibly blessed even as we bless others with our mercy. Yet it can be easier to absolve someone who wronged you, Ondrea points out, than to forgive yourself. Most of us are way harder on ourselves than we are on others. We'd sooner pardon a violent criminal whose childhood, as it turns out, was riddled with parental neglect and abuse than give ourselves a break for waking up in a bad mood and snapping at our children.

The unfinished business with which most people die, Ondrea continues, is the work of forgiveness, mostly

Photograph by Warren Wong

There is a soft, cool breeze flowing through "The Apology Page."
It feels like a safe grotto
where we can rest.

forgiveness of themselves. Ondrea told me how much she cherishes the private conversations she's had with many people as they were dying, in which they entrusted her with their deepest secrets. They needed a loving person to bear witness to these soul burdens they carried so that they could lay them down before they died. Sharing their hearts with Ondrea helped them to forgive themselves. But the exchange was not one-way. These intimate moments with the dying bestowed gifts of love Ondrea says she will keep with her until the day she dies.

A few years ago, Ondrea launched something she calls "The Apology Page" on the Levine Talks website. This is a public space where people can post anonymously, confessing the transgressions that cloud their conscience and blight their relationships. "It seems to be a very good idea as a means for tilting the shared heart and letting it pour into the ocean of compassion," Stephen and Ondrea wrote at the top of the web page. "If you were told you were completely forgiven for everything you have ever done, what is it in the heart that rejects that self-mercy? Treasure Yourselves."

The apologies range from what may appear to be minor offenses, such as envy, to significant betrayals, such as a spouse admitting to an affair. "I apologize to my mother for thinking daily about killing myself," one person writes. Some, like this one, carry remorse about actions they committed years ago: "I am sorry that, as a teenager, around fifteen years old, when I was babysitting, I left the baby alone, asleep in the house to go to a dance for a few hours." Some recognize the ways in which they have caused harm to their own dear selves:

"I apologize to myself for repressing my femininity, my desires and my feelings. I apologize to myself for believing I was valuable only if I was strong, clever and showed no feelings. I apologize to myself for striving for spiritual perfection and disregarding my humanness."

There is a soft, cool breeze flowing through "The Apology Page." It feels like a safe grotto where we can rest. Glimpsing the ways other people flagellate themselves, just as we do, can generate a couple of healing outcomes. It helps us see our participation in the universal predicament—that we are neither terminally special nor uniquely flawed—and that we belong to the human family. And the simple act of naming the ways we have missed the mark helps recalibrate our hearts and line us back up with our most loving intentions.

ALL WILL BE WELL AND ALL WILL BE WELL

The medieval English anchoress Julian of Norwich bequeathed us a radically optimistic theology. She had no problem admitting that human beings have a tendency to go astray. We rupture relationships, dishonor the Divine, make unfortunate choices, and try to hide our faults. And yet, Julian insists, "All will be well and all will be well and every kind of thing shall be well."

Take that in.

This assertion is meant to penetrate the fog of our despair and wake us up. She does not simply state, "Everything's going to be okay." Like God calling the biblical prophets by name, Julian repeats her declaration three times— most emphatically the third: All will be

Julian of Norwich. Rosalind Grimshaw, 2002. St Augustine's Church, Scaynes Hill, West Sussex, England. Photograph by Antiquary

"*I believe that sin has no substance,*"
Julian writes, "not a particle of being."

well and all will be well and every kind of thing shall be well. She does not ask us to engage in a spiritual bypass by relegating everything that unfolds to the will of God, calling it perfect against all evidence to the contrary. She squarely faces the inevitability that we will miss the mark and that there is wickedness in this world. Even so, she is convinced that the nature of the Divine is loving-kindness, and she wants us to absorb this into every fiber of our being.

In her mystical masterwork THE SHOWINGS, Julian shares that she used to obsess about sin. She couldn't figure out why God, who is all-powerful, wouldn't have eliminated our negative proclivities when he made the world. "If he had left sin out of creation, it seemed to me, all would be well." But what God-the-Mother showed Julian in a near-death vision was that all shall be well anyway. Not in spite of our transgressions but because of them.

Julian unpacks this for us. In doing so she dispenses with the whole concept of sin and replaces it with love. "I believe that sin has no substance," Julian writes, "not a particle of being." While sin itself has no existential value, it has impact. It causes pain. It is the pain that has substance. But mercy is swiftly forthcoming. It is immediately available. Inexorable! It is frankly rude of us to doubt that all will be well (and all will be well and every kind of thing shall be well). "When he said these gentle words," Julian writes, speaking of God-the-Mother, "he showed me that he does not have one iota of blame for me, or for any other person. So, wouldn't it be unkind of me to blame God for my transgressions since he does not blame me?" The merciful nature of God renders the whole blame game obsolete.

Besides, in her visions, Julian saw that we are perfectly protected. We're bound to do things we regret, whether or not we intend to, but we each carry a spark of the Holy One inside us, and this can never be extinguished. In fact, it is when we stumble that the Divine looks most tenderly upon us. Our vulnerability is beautiful to God-the-Mother.

Suffering is a purifying fire, a blessing in itself. Julian predicts that when this life is over we will understand that there is no punishment, only grace. We have already paid for our transgressions through the pain we endured as a consequence of our negative actions. In fact, we will be rewarded in direct proportion to the severity of our errors. This may seem counterintuitive, but why would a loving God, Julian asks, hold us accountable for that which we have already offered to the flames of remorse? Not only would God never allow our souls to suffer for the actions we have already accounted for in this life, but each soul is so precious to God that when she brings us home to herself she offers us the seat of honor at her own table.

For those of us who do not subscribe to a belief in some perfect afterworld but, rather, are focused on making things better right here on Earth, this teaching may feel disconnected. But what Julian is saying, with heartbreaking compassion, is that we cannot know this now, from our limited, paindrenched perspective. Yet eventually we will awaken to the truth that we are unconditionally adored by God, so that in the end, "We will clearly see in God all the secrets that are hidden from us now. Then none of us will be moved in any way to say, 'Lord, if only things had been different, all would have been well.' Instead, we shall proclaim in one voice, 'Beloved One, may you be blessed, because it is so: all is well.'"

Our task is to embody these "heavenly realms" here and now, in our relationships, in our communities, in our bedraggled and beautiful hearts.

RESTORATIVE JUSTICE

It is no surprise that many Indigenous wisdom practices echo feminine values. Native cultures are generally earth-based, and the Earth is honored as our Mother. When there is violence or discord within the collective sphere, certain tribes in Canada, the United States, Australia, and New Zealand (and undoubtedly in many other regions less documented) will gather in a circle, and the members will take turns speaking from the heart about how the incident touched them and what they think might be done to mend the torn fabric of community.

Connecting hands of restorative justice. Symbol within the Community Bridge mural project, Frederick, Maryland. Photograph by Jeff Kubina

There are so many things about this that feel feminine to me: gathering in a circle, giving space for each voice to be heard and valued, emphasizing healing over punishing. It's about rebuilding relationships.

As a result of the measurable benefits of restorative justice circles among Indigenous communities, some non-Indigenous groups have taken up this native wisdom teaching. In the classroom and the courtroom, restorative justice methods are being applied to a range of violations, from petty theft to rape, from able-bodied people parking in spots designated for the disabled (so they won't be late to football practice or some such reason) to fatal collisions caused by drunk drivers.

Here's how it works. When a crime has been committed, everyone impacted by the incident comes together in a circle. Each person affected has the opportunity to speak directly to the person responsible for the violation, sharing how they were hurt by the offender's action. The person who committed the crime also has a chance to speak. They can apologize, express their own pain and sorrow for what they did, and may begin developing a concrete plan to restore wholeness to the community.

Unlike the punitive model practiced in most Western courts, restorative justice is about repairing harm. It speaks to the whole person; it addresses and heals the soul. The philosophy underlying this process is that when someone violates the rights of an individual, they are damaging the fabric of the entire circle.

One of the most powerful experiences I've ever had—in a lifetime overflowing with powerful experiences—was sitting in a restorative justice circle. I was there in the capacity of grief counselor to a woman whose sixteen-year-old daughter had been run over by her boyfriend following a fight. They were in the parking lot of a motel where they had been partying.

When the young man entered the room where the session was to take place, his hands cuffed and his feet shackled, he did not make eye contact with anyone gathered there, including his own parents. Even after he was seated, he did not look up. Each person spoke of the ways they were impacted by the event, and at first his face was like stone. But little by little, I saw his body language begin to register what was happening around him. As the girl's basketball buddies spoke and cried, he flinched. His girlfriend's sister, who was pregnant, wept when she expressed that her dead sister would never get to be an auntie or a mom herself. Her stepfather spoke of his helplessness in the face of his wife's grief.

When the mother spoke, she did not cry. She did not hurl hateful accusations. She quietly shared the texture of her days, sleepless nights, tortured dreams, waking to remember all over again that her beautiful, feisty daughter was gone. Then, to the amazement of everyone present, she shifted her focus from her own pain to her daughter's boyfriend. She acknowledged that not only had she lost a child, but that he had lost his girlfriend. She told him that she holds him in prayer and that she might even like to visit him in prison to see how he's doing. She hoped this tragedy would inspire him to return to his community and teach boys about nonviolence. As this mighty mama shared her heart, I watched the young man's eyes fill with tears. Soon he was openly weeping. And then we were all crying: her family, his family, the district attorney, and the assistant DA. Me.

When it was my turn to speak, I encouraged the young man to use his prison sentence as a monastic opportunity—to pray and meditate, to read spiritual literature and keep his communication with fellow inmates as respectful and as kind as possible. I offered to send him books that I felt would facilitate a kind of vision quest within the desert of his incarceration: DARK NIGHT OF THE SOUL by John of the Cross, FINDING FREEDOM by Jarvis Jay Masters, WHEN THINGS FALL APART by Pema Chödrön.

After everyone had a chance to share how this incident had affected them, a blanket of collective exhaustion laced with tranquility fell over our group and rendered us momentarily mute. The facilitator skillfully allowed us to sit in this scared hush for a few minutes before closing the circle. And then the girl's mom asked if she could hug her daughter's boyfriend. The guards consented. As if in the presence of the Madonna herself, we all made way for her as she crossed the room to where stood the person responsible for her child's death, who was suddenly looking very much like a little boy.

She took him into her arms and began whispering in his ear while stroking his shaved head. His shoulders were trembling, heaving. They stayed that way, pressed together, for a long time. Then he was led away, back to jail. His sentencing followed later that week, taking into account the transformational fruits of our restorative justice process. The fabric of community had been carefully and collectively rewoven. Not a single one of us would ever be the same. ◆

Excerpted from WILD MERCY: LIVING THE FIERCE AND TENDER WISDOM OF THE WOMEN MYSTICS, by Mirabai Starr. Sounds True, April 2019. Reprinted with permission.

A warrior makes amends; a spirit crosses the sea of birth and death

Fujito

Anonymous / Japanese Noh

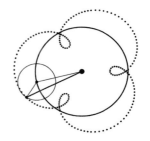

Retold by Kenneth E. Lawrence. Artwork by Kumiko Lawrence

O VER THE GENTLE WAVES they travel, rounding the islands. A gentle breeze blows through the pines; a truly joyful spring dawn. The sun rises on the shore as they reach their destination: Kojima, an island by the narrow straits of Fujito.

A retainer leaps from the ship and steps forward, addressing the gathered villagers. "Today is an auspicious day," he shouts. "Lord Saburo Moritsuna of Sasaki, the new ruler of this bay, has come to take possession of his domain! Those who hold grievances may step forward to speak!"

An elderly woman watches from a distance, her face filled with resentment. "The years, like waves, from dawn to dusk they wash over me at Fujito," she says. "With all my heart I long for the return of springs past." Lord Moritsuna, curious, motions for her to come forward. She bows, kneels before him and asks "How is it you became the new leader of this fiefdom?"

Moritsuna squares his shoulders. "I received this island as a reward for my recent victory at the battle of Fujito," he says proudly. "The straits of Fujito separated us from our foe. Some of their warriors would row out, mocking us, shouting and jeering. Unable to cross the water, we were forced to tolerate their insults. Then I found that there are two secret places where the water is shallow enough to ride across."

The woman's eyes narrow. "These two secret places, how did you come to know of them?"

Moritsuna's eyes grow distant. "One evening last year—it was the third moon, the 25th day—I spoke with a man on the shore, a fisherman. "Is there a place to get across the sea here on horseback?" I asked. "Yes," the man replied. "There is a secret place, a shifting place like the shallows of a river, the only way to cross. When the moon is new it lies to the east, when it is old it lies to the west." I plied him with gifts—a white robe, a pair of widemouthed trousers, and a dagger with a silver-wrapped hilt—and won him over.

"The fisherman and I then stole off secretly together, just the two of us. He showed me the location of the shallows and I was able to wade across.

I kept the place hidden even from my own retainers. Later, when the foe rowed out once more to taunt us, I led seven men on horseback straight into the sea. My comrades initially thought I'd lost my mind, but seeing that the water was in fact shallow, they joined me. Thousands of warriors followed, swimming their mounts across. The enemy, stunned, were driven off in a panic. Several of their overloaded boats overturned or sank in the melee.

"My fame was assured. Throughout history, many have ridden their horses across rivers, but who has ever ridden across the sea? For my meritorious service at the Battle of Fujito, I received, by written command, this island fiefdom. I have come today to claim my reward.

"But, old woman," Moritsuna says, "why do you weep so bitterly?"

"The tangles of seaweed harvested by divers are alive with creatures," she says, "beasts who, like me, cry and wail." She wipes away her tears. "The crime of a powerful warrior is, in essence, merely the revolving of Karma's wheel."

"Crime?" Moritsuna says, taken aback.

"Yes! I have come to declare your heartlessness!" The old woman rises, pointing. "You killed my son!"

"Your son, murdered?" he turns away. "I know nothing of this."

"Oh, but you do! Don't feign innocence! Concealing it is impossible, like trying to hide a mountain. Talk of my son's murder spread like weeds. You killed my son and sank his body into the depths of the sea! Pray for his spirit and his mother, who remains in this world, may perhaps find solace. I beg you to pray, please pray for his soul!"

"No, I…" he stammers. "That night, the evening moon, the waves on the shore…. Listen.

"After your son showed me the shallows, I had a sudden realization. As I turned to go, 'No, no,' I thought, 'the poor are bound to no one. What do they know of loyalty? The fisherman shared the information because of a few gifts. Others may ask him, and he might talk. This new information was such a powerful weapon, but if anyone else were to find out about the shallows, the element of surprise would be lost. The information would become useless.'

"It was cruel, but I took that man, pulled him close, and stabbed him twice, killing him. I sank his body into the sea, then returned."

"You murdered my son and sank his body into the sea…" she mutters. She turns to face the sea. "Where was the exact spot?"

Moritsuna points. "Look," he says. "There you can see a rocky sandbar. A little to this side, where the waters deepen, there I sank his dead body into the depths. A deed done by night, where evening waves roll in, the evidence deeply hidden so it wouldn't be discovered. Or so I believed."

The woman shakes her head sadly. "'Good deeds seldom go beyond the gate,' they say, 'but evil deeds roam one thousand leagues.' The rumors about that night do not differ even slightly from the truth."

"I only wished to leave my name as a valiant warrior for future generations," Moritsuna explains. "I was so very fortunate to be shown the crossing—shallows in the sea, so rare!—but if that same crossing were shown to another, what use would the information have been then? My actions, they were an act of military expediency. Anyone who calls himself a warrior would have done the same."

But the woman isn't listening. "In this life, the sad trials we must bear grow thick as bamboo along a river shore. My child…was he but a dream? For some twenty years, to part from him even briefly was torture. Will we never meet again? Send me to join him on that journey," she whispers. "Please do me this kindness." She collapses and, oblivious to the watching eyes, writhes on the ground, crying "Give me back my son!"

Moritsuna tries to calm her. "Now even regrets are in vain," he says. "But you must remember that all things, all, are from deeds done in a former life. I will pray for his soul and provide for his wife and children. Return to your home now, and clear your heart of bitterness."

Moritsuna calls to a servant and orders him to lead the woman back to her home, then "Convene the musicians!" he cries. "We shall pray for the young man's soul with a service of music. The suffering of the fisherman's mother continues, her pain still lingers, but perhaps the chanting of the sutras will guide his spirit to Buddha. Also, have the fishing nets in all the bays raised for seven days. The taking of life is forbidden. Make it known!"

For sleepless nights and days undivided in prayer, their voices, chanting Buddha's Law, float across the sea, becoming rolling waves, like drifting smoke. The Ship of Wisdom casts off its moorings, as voices rise, calming all hearts.

From the evening shadows on the water's surface, a human form emerges.

Like foam on the water I vanished, my life a mere dewdrop. Why do these feelings of sadness linger still?

I drown, descending, sinking into the desolate pathways of a darker realm that knows nothing of spring. Though my body lacks substance, some fault must have clouded the pure waters of my heart. Yet my only crime was showing the way across the sea. Though my heart is keen to forget, those hateful memories return once more.

For your prayers, I am most grateful, and yet…a bitterness unending, a resentment that clings to me still. From days long past to the present day, to cross the sea on horseback, a most rare feat! Your fame as a warrior augmented, this island your reward. If that joy was due to me, no gift of thanks would have been too great. And yet you took my life instead, a feat more rare than crossing the sea on horseback. And the memory haunts me still of how, atop the rocks of that sandbar, amid the rushing water you unsheathed your ice-like sword and stabbed it through my breast. As my soul slipped away, you pushed my body into the sea to sink a thousand fathoms deep, until the ebbing tide drew me away in its swirling waves. Sinking and resurfacing, like fossil wood I drifted, finally caught among the rocks on the ocean floor.

There, in the depths of the sea at Fujito, as if a baleful dragon, I vented my vengeful wrath. And yet—a wonder!—your prayers, their sound comforts me, leading me to board that great ship, the Ship of the Vow.

Its practiced oar rows, rapidly pulling him across the sea of birth and death. Soon his desire is fulfilled as he arrives at the other shore and, his soul released, the spirit achieves Buddhahood at last. ◆

The extraordinary mercies of the gray whales

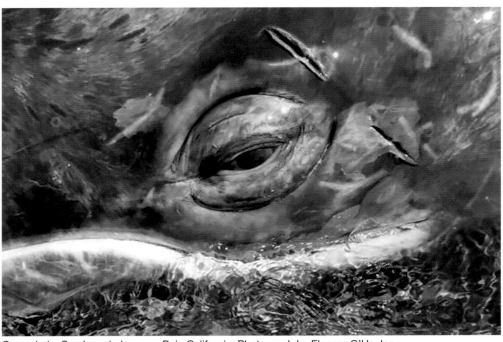

Gray whale, San Ignacio Lagoon, Baja California. Photograph by Eleanor O'Hanlon

A Gesture of Forgiveness

Eleanor O'Hanlon

WALKING ALONG THE WHITE DESERT flats crusted with black algae, I find whalebones scattered on the shore—massive shoulder blades, vertebrae, and hooped ribs. Exposure to the salt and bright sunshine, the wind and rain has worn and bleached the bones and they feel smooth and warm to the touch, as though they have taken on some of the heat of sunlight as they aged. I do not know how long they have lain here, but it is entirely possible that they once belonged to some of the whales that were slaughtered inside this lagoon.

For more than a week I have spent every day on the water among the gray whales. Every day the whales have approached with the same gentle playfulness and peace. The boats are not allowed to follow the whales. The grays themselves choose when to approach, and how long to remain alongside. I have seen some whales return to the same boat until they have connected with every single person on board. I have returned to Eden. I do not want to leave.

In recent years, some of the researchers who study cetaceans—all whales and dolphins—have begun to look at them in a much larger way. They have discovered that individual whales and dolphins have a sense of personal identity and consider the needs of others. They have the ability to use abstract concepts and communicate them to the others in their close-knit social groups. They are intensely cultural—passing information, understanding, and ideas between clans and individuals that are still mysteries to science.

The whales approach us from the other side of the human duality of guilt and forgiveness, reaching out to share that freedom with us....

As their scientific research erodes the artificial boundaries between humans and cetaceans, some leading specialists now argue that cetaceans should be granted basic rights as persons, which would mean that no whale or dolphin would ever be captured, slaughtered, or confined.

The grays themselves use a wide variety of sounds to communicate and they can live to be seventy years old. It is entirely possible that the whales that came to this lagoon in the1970s had experienced the carnage of industrial whaling, which almost wiped them completely from the Earth.

Gray whale, San Ignacio Lagoon, Baja California. Photograph by Eleanor O'Hanlon

What could possibly motivate the grays to reach out to people in this way? How can they be so open and so trusting? How can they come to us in such peace, as though they had never known that welter of blood, anguish, and death, and allow us to play with their young in the very same places where they suffered and died? These questions touch me all the more deeply because I have been with the gray whales before, at the northern end of their great annual migration. On that journey through their feeding grounds in the Bering Strait I saw the whales struck by hand-held harpoons and lances. I saw the waters of the Bering Strait run red with spurted blood from their blowholes and I saw them die. There are scientists who offer pragmatic explanations for the whales' extraordinary openness towards people. They speculate that friendly whales may be attracted by the sound of the outboard engines on the pangas, which vibrate in a similar register to their own underwater calls. Or that new mothers are looking for a way to keep their lively babies entertained and take a little time off from the demands of motherhood.

For others the whales' attitude and behavior have a profound spiritual dimension: they reach out in a gesture of forgiveness for the suffering and death they have known at human hands.

But forgiveness is a word that is loaded with the legacy of human pain, with all our emotional struggles and distress. Like anybody who has ever struggled to find forgiveness and let go of the corrosive effects of bitterness and anger, I know how these feelings linger, how they surface again after the years in which they seemed to lie forgotten. We humans hold fast to the shadows of the past; we do not find it easy to forgive.

What I have experienced among the gray whales is quite different. The whales have shared with me something of that ineffable freedom which lies beyond the difficult human struggle to forgive the past—to truly forgive both ourselves and others and find release from the repetitive cycles of pain and suffering. The whales approach us from the other side of the human duality of guilt and forgiveness, reaching out to share that freedom with us—troubled, uneasy sleepers being nudged awake by some benign, enormous friend. They are awake and present on this Earth where so many of us have gone to sleep, and lost ourselves in separate dark dreams of emptiness and fear.

In the gray whales' company I have come to realize that we do not know what the whale really is. The usual categories of understanding, based on the separation between human consciousness and the consciousness of the whale, are made meaningless by the power of their presence—life meeting life, consciousness meeting consciousness, in recognition and peace. ◆

Reprinted from Eleanor O'Hanlon's *THE EYES OF THE WILD* by kind permission of John Hunt Publishing Ltd. (www.johnhuntpublishing.com).

Photograph courtesy of Whale and Dolphin Conservation

The Lord's Prayer. John Morgan Coaley, 1889. Ink and watercolor

"I am he as you are he as you are me"
—The Beatles, "I Am the Walrus"

Why Forgive?

Richard Smoley

OR ALL THE PRAISE lavished on it, forgiveness is not easy. We often feel it as an irksome obligation, which we take on half-heartedly. How can you even be sure whether you have forgiven someone? The mind has an infinite number of nooks in which grievances can hide. You can think you've forgiven when some little irritation comes up to remind you that you've done nothing of the sort.

Then, too, much of what passes for forgiveness is little more than sanctimonious egotism. You "forgive" out of a sense of *noblesse oblige*—it is an act of condescension, a favor bestowed upon an inferior. From this position of lordliness we bestow forgiveness as we might toss a coin at a beggar.

There is another type of hypocrisy as well. It's the sort that seeks to drag everyone else into its mire, moaning, "We are all to blame." This false self-abasement likes to quote the verse from Paul, "All have sinned, and come short of the glory of God" (Rom. 3:23). So we may have—but whose agenda is it to constantly remind us of this? If it were a genuine call to humility, the one who uttered it might first apply it to himself and might then be silent. But as often expressed today—particularly in religious discourse—such declamations seek not to pardon sin but to reinforce it. Everyone is spattered indiscriminately with the spots of blame.

In one sense these difficulties are merely one more form of human frailty. But they point up the extraordinary difficulty that people often have with forgiveness. I suggest that this stems from a deeper cause: we really don't know why we should forgive. We've been told that it's the right thing to do, but *why* it might be the right thing to do is rarely addressed. Thus our efforts at forgiving are often perfunctory and insincere.

Why, then, should we forgive? The law of karma suggests one answer. A given cause has a like effect; good begets good, and evil, evil. This is self-evident. We see it every day. If a man does evil to another, he is likely to get evil in return. If a woman does a kind deed, she will probably find that kindness paid back to her.

Taken in full, this idea is sobering. "Use every man after his desert, and who shall 'scape whipping?" asks Hamlet. We know we are not innocent. If the law of karma holds, then sooner or later retribution will find us. The philosophies of India have intricate explanations for why this recompense is not instantaneous: they speak of *samskaras*, "seeds of karma" that will sooner or later blossom in the right circumstances, in this lifetime or another. Even apart from these theories, when we are aware of our guilt, we often feel the hangman is waiting.

Where, then, is the way out? Perhaps it's in forgiveness. If karma creates exact repercussions for our actions,

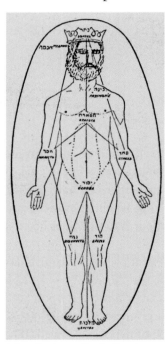

Adam Kadmon. Illustration from Brockhaus and Efron's *Jewish Encyclopedia* (1906—1913)

then by necessity it would have to wipe out our offenses to the exact degree that we wipe out those of others. As the Lord's Prayer says, "Forgive us our debts as we have forgiven our debtors" (Matt. 6:12).[1]

This verse is recited in two different ways. Sometimes it is "Forgive us our debts," sometimes "Forgive us our trespasses." Which is right? The Greek makes it extremely clear. The word is *opheilēmata*, from the verb *opheilein*, "to owe." Christ uses the word "debts" rather than "sins." In fact he speaks quite often about money and debts. In one parable, a servant (literally, "slave") owes his master ten thousand talents—a staggering, almost inconceivable amount of money, equivalent to, say, a trillion dollars today. The servant says he cannot pay, and the master forgives him. But the servant then turns around and has a "fellow servant" who owes him "a hundred pence" (or a hundred denarii, in any event a much smaller sum), cast into debtors' prison. The master then has the first servant cast into debtors' prison as well. "So likewise shall my heavenly Father do also unto you, if ye from your hearts forgive not every one his brother" (Matt. 18:23–35). To put it another way, the law of karma is inexorable. You will receive exactly what you mete out to others.

But does it really make any difference whether we speak of debts or trespasses? Actually it does. We live in a world of

If all of what passes for "my" experience is a sort of other—a film that I can watch from a distance—who or what is this mind that is doing the looking? And where is the dividing line between my mind and someone else's?

reciprocity, of transactions. We incur any number of "debts" that are not really offenses or trespasses. We may owe someone a phone call or a letter, or for that matter a greeting or a kind word. We don't always meet these obligations. The network of social exchange is so vast and intricate that it's impossible to fulfill them all. But they sit at the backs of our minds, oppressing us often without our knowledge. Christ seems to be suggesting that we need not preoccupy ourselves with these obligations in a calculating or actuarial way—so long as we're able to grant the same favor to others.

As comforting as these reflections may be, the outcome still seems rather niggling. Forgiveness may rescue us from the inexorable law of karma, but it doesn't take us past the quid pro quo of human life that turns us all into spiritual bookkeepers, keeping scrupulous records in our minds and hearts of favors and slights and injustices great and petty—what G.I. Gurdjieff called "internal considering." Even forgiveness as a means of canceling karmic debts is nothing more than an esoteric form of transactionality.

So, then, is there no way out? Not in conventional terms, whether we look at them from the perspective of biology, social obligation, family bonds, or even the comparatively esoteric

considerations of karma. In order to understand forgiveness in its deepest aspect, we need to look at reality through another dimension.

I f there is one cliché that has been constantly drummed into our ears, it is the claim that "we are all one." We hear this so often that we take it no more seriously than we do a soft-drink commercial. And why should we? There is nothing to even remotely indicate that it might be true. All over we see people jockeying for position, trying to outdo each other in money, status, comfort. One person's success means another's failure. At any given time two different people cannot be elected president, or win the Academy Award for best actress, or be the richest person in the world. One man gets the girl, the other does not. The verdict of appearances is obvious: we are *not* all one. Our name is Legion.

In what sense, then, are we all one? To answer this question, we need to look into our own experience. If we do, we'll soon see that it comes in two basic forms. There is the world of physical experience, of the outer world of the five senses. There is also the world of inner experience: thoughts, images, feelings, associations, dreams. These two worlds have been given various names in different esoteric traditions.

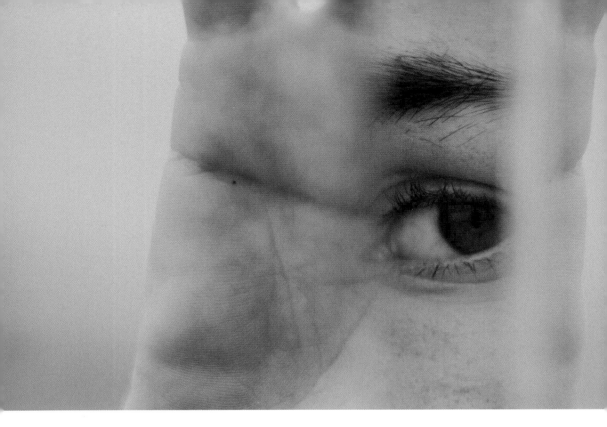

Esoteric Christianity refers to them as the body (or the "flesh") and the "soul" or "psyche" respectively. (The word in the Greek New Testament translated as "soul" is *psyche*.)

Here we have the totality of experience: body and soul, inner and outer worlds. Ancient Christianity, however, said that we are composed of *three* entities: body, soul, and spirit. Soul and spirit are two different things: "For the word of God is quick, and powerful, and sharper than any two-edged sword, piercing even to the dividing asunder of soul and spirit" (Heb. 4:12). What's the difference between the two?

While experience can be easily divided between inner and outer, between soul and body, what is left out from this duality is *that which experiences*. If there is an "I" that can witness even its own most private thoughts and desires from a remove, this "I" must be distinct from them. This is a subtle but profound

point. This witness is always *that which sees*, so of course it can never be seen. Hindu philosophy identifies this witness with the *Atman*, usually translated as "Self." The Gospels refer to it as the spirit, "the kingdom of heaven," the "kingdom of God," and "I am."

As many spiritual teachers have said, it is necessary to detach this consciousness, the true "I," from its own contents in order for liberation to occur. This is arguably what the text from Hebrews quoted above means when it speaks of the "cleaving asunder of soul and spirit." It does not refer to death but to liberation of the consciousness ("spirit") from enslavement to its own experience ("soul" or psyche). This is why practically all esoteric traditions put such emphasis on meditation, which is the day-to-day process that makes this liberation possible.

As the fixity of ordinary identification begins to dissolve, the

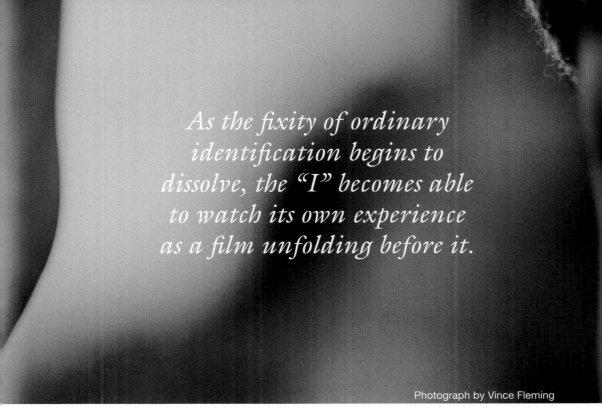

As the fixity of ordinary identification begins to dissolve, the "I" becomes able to watch its own experience as a film unfolding before it.

"I" becomes able to watch its own experience as a film unfolding before it. But then the question arises: if all of what passes for "my" experience is a sort of other—a film that I can watch from a distance—who or what is this mind that is doing the looking? And where is the dividing line between my mind and someone else's?

That is the crux of the matter. As mind begins to dissolve its attachments to its "own" experience, it begins to regard itself not as an isolated thing but as part of a larger mind. There is no real border between this "I" and the collective "I" in which we all participate. Conversely, the mind's attachment to its "own" experience causes a symbolic death in that the "I" is, or appears to be, cut off from the whole.

Countless traditions speak of this truth. Because it runs counter to what we usually regard as self-evident reality, these traditions have had to use myth or allegory to explain it. The Kabbalists sometimes speak of the Fall of Adam Kadmon, the androgynous primordial human, as a kind of dismemberment. Similarly, the Hindu *Rig Veda* (dated from 1200 to 900 B.C. or sometimes earlier) says that the universe was generated through the sacrifice and dismemberment of *purusha*, a word referring to the cosmic human but, even more profoundly, to consciousness. The Vedic hymn says:

> The Man [*purusha*] has a thousand heads, a thousand eyes, a thousand feet. He pervaded the earth on all sides and extended beyond it as far as ten fingers.

> It is the Man who is all this, whatever has been and whatever is to be. He is the ruler of immortality....

> Such is his greatness, and the Man is yet more than that. All creatures are a quarter of him; three quarters of him are what is immortal in heaven.

Tag under the Stone Arch Bridge in Minneapolis. Photograph by Tony Webster

That which is most radically the Self, the "I," *purusha*, Atman, is nothing other than this transcendent principle known as the Christ, an idea we also find in Paul: "I am crucified with Christ: nevertheless I live; yet not I, but Christ liveth in me" (Gal. 2:20). For Paul, it is neither faith nor works that saves us, but union with this cosmic Christ by realizing that the "I" that lives is the Christ that "liveth in me." What it saves us from is not the banal hell of popular imagination but the true hell of isolation from the common life that pulses throughout the universe. The "love of the world," with its accounts, transactions, and agendas, is the love of Adam in his fallen state, in which each cell of his body imagines that it is isolated and supreme and finds itself fighting for position with so many other beings who deludedly believe the same thing. It is as if the cosmic Adam had been infected with an autoimmune disease.

Agape, which could be defined as conscious love, is the love of the cosmic Christ, in which the cells of this primordial human recognize that they are joined together in a larger whole. They realize, too, that what says "I" at the deepest level in ourselves is identical to that which says "I" in everything else, human and nonhuman. This, we could say in the words of the Theosophist Annie Besant, is the "hidden light shining in every creature." To realize this truth, experientially as well as intellectually, is to achieve gnosis, to become conscious in the fullest sense.

These ideas also take us to true forgiveness, to the forgiveness that is beyond account keeping. The twentieth-century spiritual text known as *A Course in Miracles* says, "All that I give is given to myself." If ultimately there is no distinction between you and me—or, perhaps better, between "you" and "I"—then forgiveness is the only appropriate response to another being.

That which separates us is ultimately illusory, as are all imagined hurts and offenses, no matter what their nature or apparent severity. The COURSE also says, "It is sin's unreality that makes forgiveness natural and wholly sane, a deep relief to those who offer it; a quiet blessing where it is received. It does not countenance illusions, but collects them lightly, with a little laugh, and gently lays them at the feet of truth. And there they disappear entirely."

This points to one of the most common impediments to forgiveness: the belief that guilt is real and solid and therefore must belong to someone; if you take it away from another person, you are stuck with it yourself, as in the game of hot potato. We're often unwilling to forgive because we believe at some level of our minds that we will then deserve the blame: if it's not his fault, it must be mine. Put this way on paper, this is clearly an absurd belief, but as with many such beliefs, if it's allowed to hide in the recesses of consciousness, unseen and unexamined, it can wreak a great deal of havoc. True forgiveness does not transfer guilt but abolishes it.

How, then, do we forgive? Forgiveness is an art. Like all arts, it requires a subtle discrimination, a precise understanding of one's material, and a light touch that strikes the balance between inadequacy and excess. There will be times when forgiveness doesn't seem possible, when the pain felt exceeds the capacity to let it go, and our visceral impulses are all striving towards fury. This does not always happen in proportion to the offense. Sometimes we find that a powerful blow glances easily off our backs, while some all but unnoticeable grievance nags at us without cease. The emotions have their reasons, which the conscious mind does not always see, and these reasons have to be respected— at least up to a point. Forgiveness often requires steering a narrow course between nursing a grudge and pretending we have pardoned someone when we have done nothing of the kind. The chief tool needed is a rigorous inner sincerity, since the grossest forms of hypocrisy are those we practice in front of ourselves.

A practical approach toward forgiveness may involve fostering a small willingness to forgive while anger and rage burn themselves out for weeks or months. It may require drawing a line with someone—refusing to take any more abuse while also refusing to nurture any hatred on account of it. Frequently it necessitates an inner detachment, a freedom from emotional dependence on others. Sometimes it entails looking at the situation from the other people's perspective (*tout comprendre, c'est tout pardonner*, as the French say: to understand all is to forgive all). Forgiveness takes forms as diverse and unpredictable as human beings themselves. For some, generous and high-minded, it comes naturally and spontaneously, while others may find that it has to be cultivated with effort in the hard soil of their natures. It's wise to be honest with ourselves about such things, but it's also wise to remember that forgiveness is to be bestowed inwardly as well as outwardly and that a little mercy granted to ourselves often makes it easier to extend this kindness to others. ◆

[1] My translation. Many English versions render the last half of this verse as "as we forgive our debtors" or something similar, but *aphēkamen*, the verb, is in the Greek aorist tense, in this context more or less equivalent to the English perfect tense.

Vengeance or forgiveness? A grieving mother's choice

Photograph by Sunyu

In the Name of My Son

Rabbi Tirzah Firestone

IN JANUARY 2018, I spoke with Robi Damelin, a charismatic Israeli leader whose work I had been following for years. Robi is in her seventies, a striking woman with high cheekbones and short-cropped hair. In 2002, Robi's twenty-eight-year-old son David was killed by a Palestinian sniper while serving his military reserve duty at a checkpoint. Somehow she knew instantly that David's death presented her with a moral choice, a test of her integrity.

"When the army came to my door to tell me that David had been killed, apparently the first thing I said was, '*You may not take revenge in the name of my son!*'" Robi said. "It was totally instinctive. I saw then that I had a choice about what to do with my pain—to invest it in revenge or try to think creatively.

"David was a student at Tel-Aviv University doing a masters in the philosophy of education. When he was called up to the reserves, he came to talk to me. 'What shall I do?' he asked, because he was in such a quandary.... But then he went, and I was filled with dread.

"He was murdered by a Palestinian sniper who, as a child, had seen his uncle killed very violently. So this man went on a path of revenge and unfortunately, David was in the way, along with nine other people.

"After [David] was killed, I was beside myself with grief. Friends from all over Israel arrived with food and drink and other little expressions of love."

Because Robi worked in Tel Aviv in public relations, word of her loss was passed on quickly, along with her declaration about revenge. Members of the Parent Circle-Families Forum (PCFF) took notice and shortly thereafter, the group's founder, Yitzhak Frankenthal, got in touch. The organization soon became her lifeline.

A few years later, Israeli army officials again knocked at Robi's door. This time they brought a message that the IDF had caught the sniper who had killed David. They asked if she wanted to attend his trial.

"I said no, because what was the point? Would it bring back David if I felt good about the fact that this man was rotting in jail and his mother is sitting alone without him? I don't believe in revenge because what revenge could I take to bring David back?

"But I am also very reluctant to use the word 'forgiving.' Does forgiving mean giving up your right to justice? Does it mean that what they did was okay, or that they can do it again? Or do you forget? I simply don't know."

Robi decided to write a letter to the family of David's killer telling them that he was a peace activist who struggled with having to serve in the occupied Palestinian territories. It was delivered to them by two Palestinian friends of hers. There was no response. And then, two and a half years later, she received a letter from David's killer himself through the Palestinian news service.

"It was not exactly a letter written by Martin Luther King," Robi said. "It was a letter filled with hate and justification for killing, telling me that my own son was a murderer. The sniper said he didn't want me anywhere near his family and would not write to me directly.

"The letter upset me terribly. But I also realized through this process that I was no longer a victim, depending upon the Palestinian sniper. The path of reconciliation brought peace to my life."

"You know, the pain doesn't go away," Robi mused. "You could take anything and everything away from me, if I could only see David one more time. I think of him all the time. At the place where he is buried, the parents make beautiful gardens around the graves of their loved ones. I see it as a continuation of motherhood, the enduring need to tend to your child."

In addition to being a spokeswoman for PCFF, Robi belongs to an international organization called the Forgiveness Project.[1] And she has traveled back to her native South Africa to study the social structures that helped make reconciliation possible after fifty years of apartheid. Robin wondered if perhaps some form of that country's Truth and Reconciliation could be applied to the Israeli-Palestinian conflict. While she was there, she met a woman named Ginn whose daughter had been brutally murdered twenty years earlier.

"Ginn helped me find forgiveness. She explained that forgiveness for her is 'giving up her just right for revenge.' After Ginn forgave the man responsible for killing her daughter, he told her that her forgiveness had released him from the prison of his inhumanity."

Ironically, Robi returned to Israel to learn that the Palestinian sniper who had killed David was on the list of one thousand Palestinian prisoners "with blood on their hands" who were to be freed in exchange for the safe return of one Israeli soldier.[2]

"Once again, I was faced with a test to see if I am honest and I mean what I say," Robi said. "I sequestered myself for three days to grapple with this test. I came out knowing that David is not coming back. That no matter how many prisoners are released or kept incarcerated, David was not coming back. I know that a prisoner exchange is part of any peace agreement. This is the way it has been the world over. This is the way for Israel, too." ◆

[1] The Forgiveness Project is dedicated to awareness, education, and transformation through the use of real stories of victims and perpetrators to explore concepts of forgiveness and to encourage people to consider alternatives to resentment, retaliation, and revenge. For more information about the Forgiveness Project, see http://the forgivenessproject.com.

[2] Gilad Shalit is a former MIA solider of the IDF who was captured by Hamas militants on June 25, 2006 in a cross-border raid near the Israeli border. Hamas held Shalit captive for over five years, until his release on October 18, 2011, as part of a prisoner exchange deal.

Reprinted here from WOUNDS INTO WISDOM: HEALING INTERGENERATIONAL JEWISH TRAUMA (2019) by Rabbi Tirzah Firestone, Ph.D. , by kind permission of Monkfish Book Publishing Company, Rhinebeck, New York

To Forgive

Desmond Tutu

The following is excerpted from the website of The Forgiveness Project. For more information, please visit www.theforgivenessproject.com.
—The Editors

To FORGIVE IS NOT JUST TO BE ALTRUISTIC. It is the best form of self-interest. It is also a process that does not exclude hatred and anger. These emotions are all part of being human. You should never hate yourself for hating others who do terrible things: the depth of your love is shown by the extent of your anger.

However, when I talk of forgiveness I mean the belief that you can come out the other side a better person. A better person than the one being consumed by anger and hatred. Remaining in that state locks you in a state of victimhood, making you almost dependent on the perpetrator.

If you can find it in yourself to forgive then you are no longer chained to the perpetrator.

You can move on, and you can even help the perpetrator to become a better person too.

But the process of forgiveness also requires acknowledgement on the part of the perpetrator that they have committed an offence. I don't like to talk about my own personal experience of forgiveness, although some of the things people have tried to do to my family are close to what I'd consider unforgivable. I don't talk about these things because I have witnessed so many incredible people who, despite experiencing atrocity and tragedy, have come to a point in their lives where they are able to forgive. ◆

Healing visions of the Heart Sutra

Mandala of Evolution. Iwasaki Tsuneo

Painting Enlightenment

Paula Arai / Artwork by Iwasaki Tsuneo

THE EXTRAORDINARY PAINTINGS *on the next several pages were begun at age seventy by Iwasaki Tsuneo (1917-2002), a retired Japanese research biologist. Iwasaki, who fought for his country during WWII, was raised as a Buddhist and pursued Buddhist studies throughout his life, finally choosing the Heart Sutra as his principal focus.*

The Heart Sutra, author unknown, dates to the seventh century A.D. and is considered a core text of Mahāyāna Buddhism. The sutra comments on the fundamental emptiness of all phenomenon. Its most famous formulation is "Form is emptiness; emptiness is form. Form is not different from emptiness; emptiness is not different from form."

In retirement, Iwasaki spent years studying calligraphy, and at age sixty-three took up the traditional practice of scripture-copying, reproducing the Heart Sutra in calligraphy nearly two thousand times. At age seventy, he applied his now expert calligraphic skills to the great array of paintings that are sampled in these pages and that unite with great insight and originality both spiritual and scientific understanding.

The meticulous attention and passionate devotion invested by Iwasaki in these paintings is evident in every brush stroke. For his ink, he did not add simple tap water to his ink stick; rather, each year, on the seventh day of the seventh month, he collected dewdrops from lotus flowers, using this liquid for his ink. His brushes ranged from ten hairs wide to three hairs wide. He painted on washi *(traditional Japanese fibrous paper) through a magnifying glass; the works range in size up to the seventeen-foot-wide* Big Bang: E=mc2. *Each work depicts the Heart Sutra within its borders.*

Iwasaki's work—here presented with commentary by scholar Paula Arai—has gained in appreciation and renown since his death. The Dalai Lama has blessed it. May we all benefit from it.

—The Editors

RAINBOW OF FORGIVENESS

Rainbow of Forgiveness. Iwasaki Tsuneo

What can I do if I forgive?

It was not until after retiring from research on viruses that Iwasaki saw he had divided reality up by looking at it only through his scientific perspective. He felt mortified that he had not treated with respect the animals that supported his research, only seeing them as things to measure. He looked mournful as he explained how this painting was his expression of repentance from his estranged way of relating to his animal research subjects. He wanted to focus on reality in its wholeness. Contemplating nonduality—that ultimately there is no subject and object—released guilt and shame that constricted him. As his heart became unbound, penetrating gratitude flowed to the animals that had helped him, especially silkworms. Gratitude helped him see reality in its wholeness, and forgiveness helped him return to wholeness.

Squarely facing this reality, he paints himself in hell to assist the animals out of the realm of suffering to which he had conscripted them. With an exultant awareness that research animals are integral to the greater whole, he entrusts the beauty of a rainbow to convey his gratitude and to celebrate opening his heart to our wholeness. Effulgent with HEART SUTRA wisdom on the interrelated nature of existence, Iwasaki's *Rainbow of Forgiveness* accentuates forgiveness as an act of compassion to the self, which activates compassion for others.

RINGING BELL

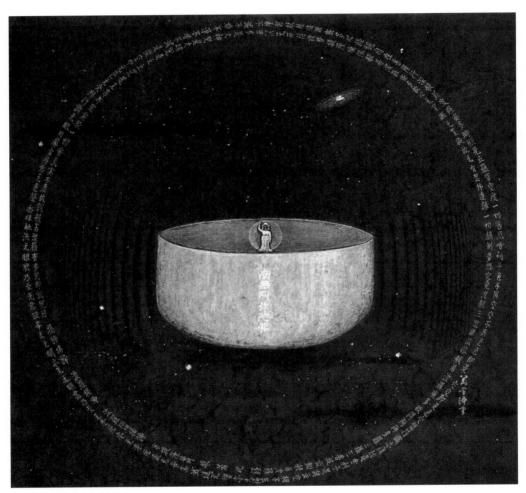

Ringing Bell. Iwasaki Tsuneo

How do I make my heart ring with compassion? Summoning the bodhisattva of compassion, Kannon—whose name in Japanese means "see sound"—Iwasaki shows us sound waves resounding into the cosmos, echoing the spiraling galaxy. Signified by *ensō* circles, the waves ripple with the teachings of the *Heart Sutra*. The baby Buddha brims with the timbre of growth. Carved in gold, "Namu Amida Butsu" heralds the vow of compassion embedded in each toning of the bell.

After his mother passed away, Iwasaki continued her morning ritual of lighting a candle, offering incense, and ringing the home altar bell before chanting. Tolling a bell in your home bathes the inhabitants in currents of calming compassion and suffuses the home with the sound of wisdom. Listening to a bell with our heart creates a space safe for dissolving debris, unclogging lines of connection, and dispelling clouds that obscure our vision. Subtle and nimble, the sound waves infuse each sliver and crack in the heart with the healing that comes from being made whole with the fullness of the present moment. Here, world peace does not sound naïve. The voice of justice does not ring hollow. Ritually intoning a bell enables us to hear the complex harmonies of the cosmos as one moves through one's day attuned to the *Heart Sutra*.

COMPASSION RIPPLES

Compassion Ripples. Iwasaki Tsuneo

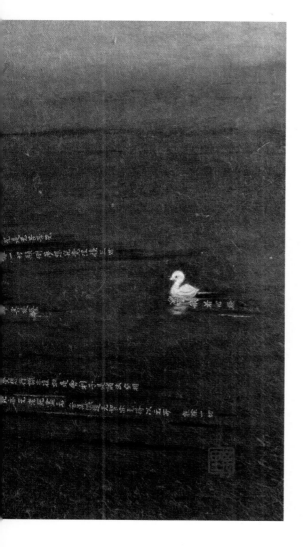

How am I held in love? Cradled in blue, a brood of ducklings swims in the protective wake of *Heart Sutra* ripples that their mother radiates as she looks lovingly aft. Embracing her young and vulnerable charges, she quells their fears and tends to their growth. In *Compassion Ripples*, Iwasaki shows us what a compassionate relationship between parent and child looks like. Iwasaki ached that not everyone knows such compassion. He penned his pain, "Saddened to live in a time when people are lost and in an age where parents kill children and children kill parents." This painting is a prayer for compassion. Seeds of compassion are watered with each intimate connection. Compassion generates inspiring and empowering energy. Parents embody compassion when they nurture compassion in their children. Suffering ceases when we experience the universe as a vast interdependent web where we are all parents and we are all children. ◆

From *Painting Enlightenment: Healing Visions of the Heart Sutra* by Paula Arai © 2019 by Paula K. R. Arai, Ph.D. Reprinted in arrangement with Shambhala Publications, Inc. Boulder, CO. www.shambhala.com

Photograph by Eberhard Grossgasteiger

God's greatest and most powerful quality

Mercy

Lee van Laer

MERCY HAS INTRICATE LINGUISTIC ROOTS. In Latin, the word *merced* meant *reward*; in later Christian Latin, *heavenly reward* or *pity*. Now, pity implies compassion and a caring for the sorrow of another. Pity, in turn, derives from piety, Latin *pietas*, or pius. This in turn means to be dutiful.

It's quite the word salad. I think we can safely say that the idea that the Lord might pity us (care for our fallen state of sin and suffering) is a core meaning in today's Christian practice; we earnestly wish to be forgiven for our transgressions against a higher, sacred principle.

Yet this is a conceptual approach. What's the nature of experience?

In practical terms, Mercy isn't just an idea or a concept; in its metaphysical and esoteric sense, it's a substance.

That is to say, it's of a material nature, and we human beings have the potential to participate in the sensation of that tangible substance. We can *receive* Mercy—else why ask for it? This understanding is entirely consistent with the idea that it can be bestowed; and it brings it out of the realm of the theological or philosophical and into the realm of the personal.

One can *personally* ask for help from a higher level; *and that help can be bestowed and received*. This is an essential premise in the invocation of the classic prayer:

Lord, have Mercy.

Sénanque Abbey, 1987. Gordes, France. Photograph by Ziegler175

The prayer, of itself, assumes by default the personhood of both the divine and the human; it thus, whether by accident or intention, implies the union of the divine and the human in Christ, by means of the exchange between both natures. An exchange between beings.

Although Mercy is a metaphysical substance—its rate of vibration is higher than that of the coarse material plane of existence we live within and sense— its vibrations can be actively received within being as a substance that concentrates in the body.

On a visit to Sénanque several years ago, a Catholic woman who had participated in several retreats there (Sénanque is one of the very few still-active ancient Cistercian abbeys in the world which allows lay visitors to participate) said:

"When you pray here for some days with the monks, you begin to *feel God in the body.*"

She said this with a sense of awe and wonder appropriate to the experience, which is the truth: one can *feel God in the body.*

This is the sensation of Mercy as it flows downward into Being and is received by the devout. It's an experience hard-won and only available, for the most part, under what we'd call "special" circumstances; if it matures, one experiences what Paul called "the peace of God which passes all understanding." Yet for all of our secular and philosophical musings about mercy in its many temporal forms—often associated with strictly human institutions such as the justice system—it's the encounter with this metaphysical manifestation of Mercy as a flow of Grace into Being that truly reveals its dimension as an inner force.

The existence of Mercy as a substantial force, not a concept, thought, or outer action, marks the division between our understanding of what is sacred and what is ordinary. Mercy, according to the Sufis, is God's greatest and most powerful quality, which exceeds all other aspects of His Being. In the midst of the suffering that inevitably arises throughout material creation, it's the one force made universally available to help alleviate the terrifying consequences of existence, with all that it implies. As the prime emanation of God's true Being, it offers us a direct contact.

Human beings are created with the capacity to open our inner being to the receipt of this flow of Mercy. To do so is one of the inner aims of the religious life. Its actions are understood to be deeply transformational; yet like the peace it bestows, it passes all understanding—everything the intellectual mind can offer.

What irony, perhaps, that we have to come to it through the intellect. Yet beginning there, if the mind is sufficiently stilled, and we wait quietly in silence, intimately sensing our bodies as the sacred vessels they are—then some particle of Mercy may touch us, no matter how lightly or swiftly, and remind us not just of our mortality, but of the Grace which is always and forever available to support us.

If we're even quieter and more attentive, some tiny portion may stay to inform us as we move outward, back into our daily life.

This is the mustard seed, and from that seed great plants grow. ◆

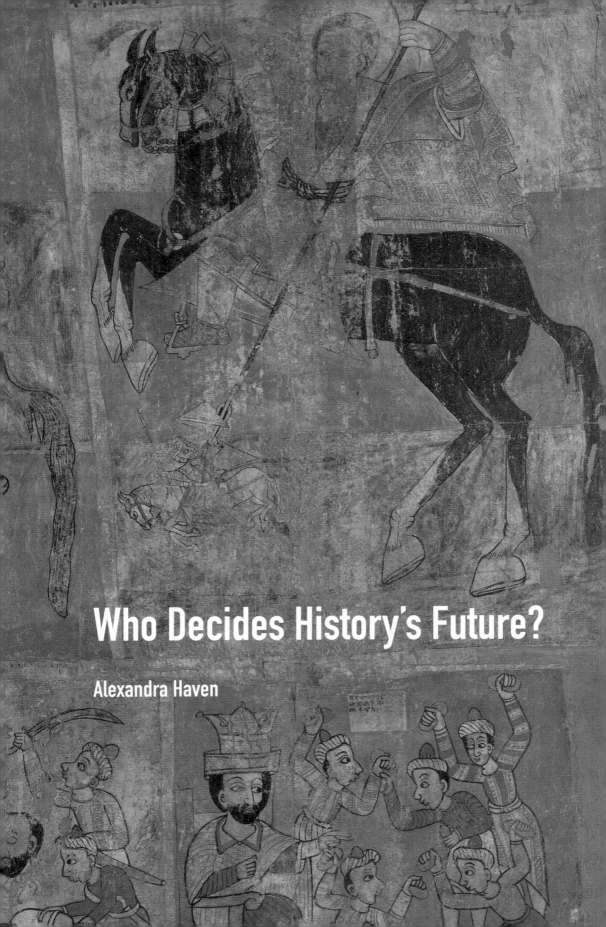

Who Decides History's Future?

Alexandra Haven

Knights and martyrs. Painting (detail) on canvas from church
of Abbas Antonios, Ethiopia. Late seventeenth century. Musée
du quai Branly-Jacques Chirac, Paris

Of might and right, and the future of the world's art

IN THE ERA OF PRINCES, Abyssinia had no king.
It had an emperor in name alone, locked in his fortress to the
north. He wore a crown of gold and bore the blood of King
Solomon, but he did not rule. Instead, he was ruled by his regent, who
in turn tried to rule over the warring princes spread across the land.

Abyssinia knew no peace.

One of those princes lost his title when he lost his father. He fled his
homeland, known as "the taste of honey," for school where he learned
poetry, history, and the art of war. But his new home fell under the rule
of another prince and he ran once more, lest he lose his head like he
lost his crown.

With the cunning he had learned, the prince became an outlaw and
the master of an army. He soon caught the eye of the emperor's regent,
who offered the emperor's granddaughter to the prince as a wife,
hoping to bind this warrior to the line of Solomon.

But our prince had two secrets.

First, there was the prophecy: it was said that one day a prince would
return greatness to Abyssinia as a true ruler over a united kingdom.

Second, there was the blood: he too was a son of King Solomon.

Our prince would see himself shrouded in myth. And so the prince
of poetry and war overthrew the men in power and became the true
Emperor of Abyssinia.

His rule spread like wildfire, pushing the very boundaries of the
kingdom. He built alliances with those in Abyssinia and those far away,
and all sent tribute to this promised prince. Even the most powerful
queen in the world gifted him a pistol, gleaming metal and wood.

He wanted that modernity lit by gunpowder for Abyssinia, but
his borders were a shifting line, rebels within and without. Soon, the
prince needed help. He wrote to the kingdoms beyond the sea, his
hope lying with his friend, the powerful queen.

But no help came. The prince's patience grew thin. He locked up
subjects of that fateful queen, hoping to get her attention. Surely she
would not abandon a fellow servant of Christ.

He succeeded. The queen noticed and sent her armies to invade
Abyssinia. The emperor released his prisoners, but the queen promised
him only life in captivity.

He was a promised prince. His myth could not end in a cage.

On Easter Monday, April 13, 1868, Emperor Tewodros II shot himself with Queen Victoria's gift pistol. His became a new myth: one of an independent Ethiopia outside the control of imperial Europe.

Still, the British armies came, torching his fortress and churches and looting as the city burned to ash. It took fifteen elephants and two hundred mules to carry the bounty to their ships.

One British soldier cut off two locks of the emperor's hair while painting his deathbed portrait and brought them home to England. The emperor's son, Prince Alemayehu, was also taken as a souvenir, first in the care of the explorer Tristam Charles Sawyer Speedy and later of Queen Victoria herself. She loved the boy and was devastated upon news of his death at age eighteen, when he died alone in the cold Yorkshire moors.

Tewodros II, c. 1860.

"It is too sad!" she wrote in her diary. "All alone, in a strange country, without a single person or relative belonging to him…. Everyone is sorry."[1]

The story of Emperor Tewodros II is all but forgotten in Britain, but in Ethiopia, his legend is one of epic proportions. Plays, songs, and memory have kept Tewodros alive in the Ethiopian canon. But the loot from the British Expedition to Abyssinia and the aftermath of Tewodros's suicide still largely remains in British collections.

In March 2019, however, locks of hair taken from the emperor were finally returned and reinterred at his tomb in Ethiopia. In a powerful ceremony in London, the cultural minister for Ethiopia, Dr. Hirut Kassaw, received the locks, proclaiming that "for

Ethiopians, these are not simply artifacts or treasures, but constitute a fundamental part of the existential fabric of Ethiopia and its people."[2]

Terry Dendy, Head of Collections Standards and Care at the National Army Museum, where the locks had been held since the mid-twentieth century, explained the decision in a brief letter to the public:

"Having spent considerable time researching the provenance and cultural sensitivities around this matter, we believe the Ethiopian government claim to repatriate is reasonable and we are pleased to be able to assist. Our decision to repatriate is very much based on the desire to inter the hair within the tomb alongside the Emperor."[3]

In a letter meant to be merciful, there is the edge of an imperial sword. This was a decision for Britain to make, not Ethiopia. But to whom should the emperor belong?

The West is wrestling with its colonial heritage in the most literal sense: its museums teem with treasure taken on conquests abroad. Crowns and swords, books and bones. The breadth of culture ripped from its home is hard to comprehend, as is the sheer scale of it: ninety percent of Africa's art is held on other continents.

Imagine the Liberty Bell gone, Versailles stripped of its Hall of Mirrors, the Roman Forum empty of columns and stones. To see them, you would have to travel across seas, deserts, mountains; apply for visas and buy a ticket for a glance at your people's history behind glass. Spread that theft to Asia, the Americas, and even other corners of Europe. The scope is unimaginable, as are the emotional scars left by the absence of national treasures.

"This is not just about the return of African art," Prince Kum'a Ndumbe III of Cameroon explains. "When someone's stolen your soul, it's very difficult to survive as a people."[4]

The question of what to do with objects collected during the colonial period is gaining traction with those beyond museum curators. Around the time of the return of Tewodros's hair, President Emmanuel Macron of France announced, "I cannot accept that a large part of the cultural heritage of several African countries is in France," and declared that the return of colonial collections would be a priority for his government.[5]

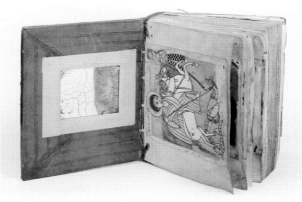

King Theodore's [Tewodros's] Bible. Manuscript written on vellum, tooled leather binding. Wellcome Library, London

While many see it as a moral or philosophical question, the repatriation of collections is also a legal one: many governments have laws preventing the breakup of national collections, no matter their provenance.

There have been several attempts to work around this. Some have turned to loans, by which objects can be put in displays in their country of origin while technically still belonging to colonial power who took it. Though not a perfect solution, it offers a first step for many people to reclaim their history.

But it is not only treasure that was taken, as seen in the case of Tewodros's hair. Groups from around the world are campaigning for the bodily remains of their ancestors to be returned to their rightful resting places. In America, the leggings and hair of Sitting Bull were returned by the Smithsonian to the Native American leader's descendants in 2007 after years of campaigning.[6] Across the world, museums and scientific collections are being pressed to return the remains of Indigenous Australians, many of whom were disinterred for research up through the 1940s.[7]

Items of spiritual significance are also at the heart of these fights. The Rapa Nui people of the Easter Islands have been campaigning for the return of their world-famous moai, or Easter Island head statue, which currently stands in the British Museum. The moai represents a deified ancestor and is believed to have brought peace to the island a thousand years ago.

"It embodies the spirit of an ancestor, almost like a grandfather. This is what we want returned to our island—not just a statue," explains Carlos Edmunds, the president of the Council of Elders.[8] The pain in its absence can be felt in the statue's name: "Hoa Hakananai'a," meaning lost friend. It was renamed after the British took it in 1868.

But there are many who oppose the repatriation of collections. Museums turn to provenance to support their claim to items, pointing to the legality by which they were purchased. The most famous case is that of the Parthenon Marbles, which were collected by Lord Elgin in Athens and are currently housed in London. While Greece continues to demand their return, the British Museum argues that Lord Elgin collected them "with the full knowledge and permission of the Ottoman authorities."[9]

Others worry about the safety of objects if moved from their current homes. Museums can be looted or burned down, as was the case of the National Museum of Brazil in 2018, where as much as ninety percent of the collection was destroyed. We must protect the world's heritage. Would returning objects threaten their survival?

There is one argument against repatriation that stands out amongst the others: those from both sides of the discussion who want only some work repatriated, while other pieces remain in the world's most eminent museums alongside Western masters. Sent back home, heritage might be forgotten, but next to Rodin, Da Vinci, and O'Keefe, all countries may be seen on the world stage. The British Museum uses this argument in their claim over the Parthenon Marbles, highlighting that if returned to Athens the statues would be "appreciated against the backdrop of Athenian history" while in London they are "an important representation of ancient Athenian civilisation in the context of world history."[10]

Are the world's top museums, then, the curators of worth?

There is no question that museums do important, irreplaceable work, and that far from all collections are built from stolen goods. But as we begin to question who owns the past, more questions arise about museums' role in the current world climate. Are they the rightful guardians of our heritage? Or are they the last bastion of empire, clinging to treasure under the guise of a moral code?

Many of the arguments against repatriation echo with racist tones, like that of the safety of objects. New museums are being built across the world, like Museum of Black Civilizations in Senegal, to modern, safe standards. It is true that the museum burned in Brazil, but so did Notre Dame in Paris. Can anywhere truly promise survival for these ancient artifacts?

Similarly, the legality of purchase is questionable if one side was a conquering force backed by the strength of an empire. What fair agreement can be made with with a war machine in the negotiations?

There is forgiveness to be sought in these great museums, but beyond them, too.

One misty spring day in England, during her visit to collect Emperor Tewodros II's hair, Minister Kassaw stood silently in the catacombs of Windsor Castle, a wreath laid by her feet. Nearby, a brass plaque reads, "I was a stranger and ye took me in."

She stood for minute's silence in honor of Emperor Tewodros II's son, Prince Alemayehu, who is buried in the castle's St. George's Chapel amongst the kings and queens of England.[11] Since 2007, Ethiopia has requested the return of his body so that he might be interned alongside his father, but so far they remain rebuffed by Queen Elizabeth II, who says that while she sympathizes, the prince cannot be exhumed without disturbing the sanctity of the others buried with him.[12]

There is no easy path to heal the trauma of our entangled histories, so intertwined by the brutal reign of empires that our dead share the same grave. But there is a reckoning upon us that we cannot ignore: to whom does history belong? And who will choose its future? ◆

[1] "Prince Alamayu." Royal Collection Trust, 2019, www.rct.uk/collection/themes/trails/black-and-asian-history-and-victorian-britain/prince-alamayu.

[2] "Ethiopians cheer as London museum returns plundered royal hair." Reuters, 2019, https://af.reuters.com/article/topNews/idAFKCN1R-21BV-OZATP?feedType=RSS&feedName=topNews.

[3] "National Army Museum responds to repatriation request from Ethiopia." National Army Museum, 2019, https://www.nam.ac.uk/press/national-army-museum-responds-repatriation-request-ethiopia.

[4] "Return of African Artifacts Sets a Tricky Precedent for Europe's Museums." NEW YORK TIMES, 2018, https://www.nytimes.com/2018/11/27/arts/design/macron-report-restitution-precedent.html.

[5] "France urged to change heritage law and return looted art to Africa." GUARDIAN, 2018, https://www.theguardian.com/world/2018/nov/21/france-urged-to-return-looted-african-art-treasures-macron.

[6] "Smithsonian Returns Sitting Bull Relics." NEW YORK TIMES, 2007, https://www.nytimes.com/2007/09/18/arts/design/18arts-SMITHSONIANR_BRF.html

[7] "The bone collectors: a brutal chapter in Australia's past." GUARDIAN, 2014, https://www.theguardian.com/world/2014/jun/14/aboriginal-bones-being-returned-australia

[8] "Easter Islanders call for return of statue from British Museum." GUARDIAN, 2019, https://www.theguardian.com/culture/2019/jun/04/easter-islanders-call-for-return-of-statue-from-british-museum.

[9] "The Parthenon Sculptures." British Museum, 2019, https://www.britishmuseum.org/about_us/news_and_press/statements/parthenon_sculptures.aspx.

[10] ibid

[11] "Ethiopia Requests Remains of Prince Alemayehu." ALLAFRICA, 2019, https://allafrica.com/stories/201903260747.html.

[12] "Give back our stolen prince, Your Majesty: The Queen sparks diplomatic row by rejecting Ethiopia's plea to return 'lost king' buried 140 years ago at Windsor Castle." DAILY MAIL, 2019, https://www.dailymail.co.uk/news/article-7018909/

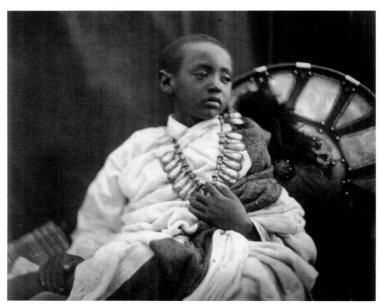

Déjatch Alámayou, King Theodore's son and heir to Emperor Theodore of Abyssinia, 1868. Photograph by Julia Margaret Cameron

Photograph by Dane Wetton

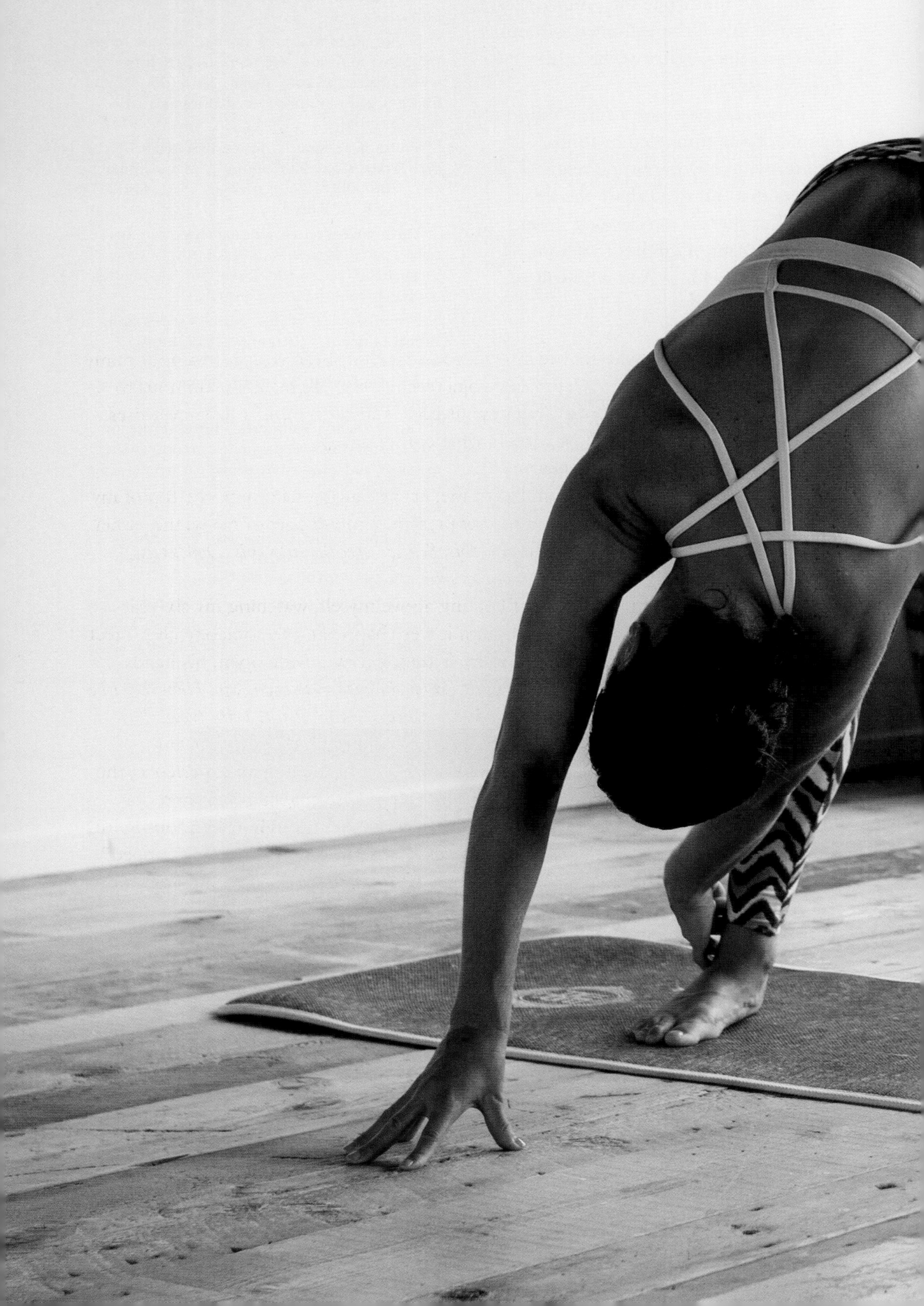

The Toughest Spiritual Practice

Seane Corn

B REATHING INTO MY SMELLY YOGA MAT, my head resting in a pool of my sweat, I hear Bryan, my yoga teacher, say, "Remain equanimous to your experience. Stay in your body and be present to whatever rises. Try not to judge it. Just witness what comes up...."

Stay in my body? Be present?

Anxiety, a feeling so familiar to me, keeps clawing its way to the top of my awareness. Although I want to stay present, another part of me would rather dissociate. *No,* I think. *Stay with this, Seane. Breathe into this. Don't run, please! What does your body want to say?*

I remember that feeling of floating above myself, watching my six-year-old body being touched, as though it were happening to someone else. I feel so sad for that poor girl lying there frozen, her eyes wide open, his hands between her legs. I think to myself, *My body has never been safe. How can I be present? If I'm present, I have to do something, and I can't. I am frozen!*

Bryan continues to move through the room reminding us that our bodies have wisdom. He speaks of the fragility of the human experience, the challenges we all face, and the ways in which these challenges expand our perspective and open our hearts ... if we allow them to. He talks about Spirit, self-love, equanimity, and the importance of letting the emotions "trapped" inside of us out so they no longer have power. He speaks of vulnerability, of surrender, and of acceptance.

He then says something about forgiveness.

My body tightens and rage rips through me once again. *Forgiveness? Are you kidding me? F- you!* I scream in my head, silently addressing my molester. I am surprised by the intensity of my reaction. My anger scares me, and I start to shake. How deep does this rage go? Then, as though reading my mind, Bryan suggests to the class: "Start with yourself. Forgive yourself for thinking you should have known better."

Forgive myself? My whole body releases into the floor. The tension melts away. My eyes open, and I stare at the floor in front of me.

I exhale fully.

*The truth is that we are
here to awaken to the light,
to the God within us
and within all.*

Photograph by Dane Wetton

I let myself see the beautiful girl that I had been, and I feel an enormous amount of compassion for this bright and sensitive soul. I realize how deeply her story lives in my body, and I see all the ways in which I have managed to control the physical and emotional discomfort that has never really gone away. I knew I was angry, deeply angry, and that this anger has been with me a long, long time. I also knew that I have avoided this anger, and the grief beneath it, by running away from it in different ways over all these years. In that moment, I realize that by running away from my grief, I have also abandoned the tenderest parts of myself and left her, my little self, behind. I make a silent commitment to myself that I will never abandon or betray the little girl within me again. I know I have a lot of work ahead of me, but I want to protect her and give her a voice and hear what she needs to say. "I am so sorry," I say to her and to my body. I have learned how to cope, but now I want to learn how to heal. I haven't a clue how to do that, but I know that I must, and I will. "I am so sorry," I repeat again and again.

To forgive is probably the toughest spiritual practice we will face in life. But forgive we must in order to release the caustic energy festering within us, making us sick, and separating us from our highest Self—and from each other. Forgive because we recognize that we are all flawed, all broken to some degree, all traumatized, all human. Ignore the story and see the soul. The people who have hurt us may be assholes, but they are also children of God, like we all are.

So give them back to God. Pray they learn, heal, and open to love. It is this forgiveness that unites, and it is this forgiveness that heals. And just when you think you've fully forgiven, forgive again. This process takes time, but it's worth it; in the end, you get your Self back. Fully and whole.

I could not transcend suffering until I forgave my molester and every other harasser, manipulator, and abuser. Forgiving them never once meant that I condoned their behavior. Not even a little bit. Forgiveness means I refuse to carry them, their energy, their wounds, and their story within me. As long as I stay stuck in the story, bound to them in negativity, I can never break free. Our commingled pain will continue to influence my present and my future choices and keep me disconnected from my truth.

The truth is that we are here to awaken to the light, to the God within us and within all. How do we do that? By experiencing all of life, without creating separation. By healing the fractured parts of ourselves and accepting the gifts every one of our relationships has to give. By seeing the soul of every being as a pure expression of that person's own divinity. Finally, by letting ourselves love the whole messy, chaotic, and beautiful process of "being" that can bring us home to the God within. ◆

Excerpted from *REVOLUTION OF THE SOUL: AWAKEN TO LOVE THROUGH RAW TRUTH, RADICAL HEALING, AND CONSCIOUS ACTION,* by Seane Corn. Sounds True, September 2019. Reprinted with permission.

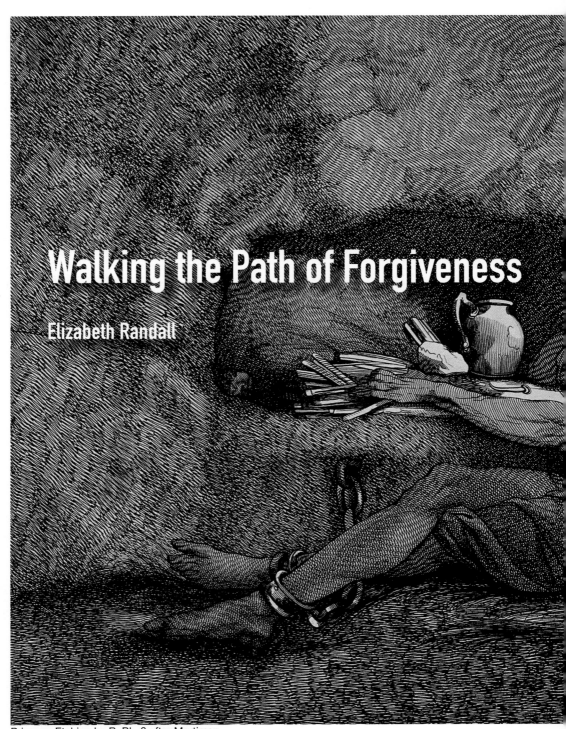

Walking the Path of Forgiveness

Elizabeth Randall

Prisoner. Etching by R. Bl...? after Mortimer

He's on death row. She gives him books, and he helps her to forgive.

YEARS AGO I wrote about a horrible murder case for a local alternative newspaper. I was the only reporter the murderer would talk to, and we had several interviews, sitting across from each other, divided by bullet-proof glass, speaking into telephones. It occurs to me, seventeen years later, that one of the reasons I still communicate with Troy Victorino, the convicted murderer and presumed ringleader of the Florida X-box murders, is a benign one.

I send him books. Usually, they're books he requests. But sometimes they're my own opinion about what he should read. For example, after getting into my car after working out yesterday, I grabbed my phone and impulsively ordered THE SUN DOES SHINE. The book is an Oprah's Book of the Month pick about an Alabama man of color who was wrongly convicted of a double murder and spent fourteen years in prison before incontrovertible evidence of his innocence emerged.

Why would I send that to Troy? There is no doubt he is guilty of the crime for which he was convicted: beating six adults to death with a baseball bat because they stole an X-box he'd left at a house where he was squatting. But the book will fit his view of his own narrative, and I thought it wouldn't hurt for him to get the perspective of a real victim of justice.

My point is, I get to dictate some of Troy's reading matter, and on death row, books are practically a convict's only lifeline. As an English teacher, I see an opportunity to mold Troy's hardened criminal mind while appealing to his more civilized inclinations. And he's literally a captive audience to my literary tastes.

He reads everything I send him, including A TALE OF TWO CITIES and THEIR EYES WERE WATCHING GOD. He also likes murder mysteries, like those by David Baldacci, and spy stories. He likes juvenile fantasy because he has a daughter, although he hasn't seen her in years, who reads Rick Riordan.

Doing good assuages, even a little bit, the essential wrongness of the world. It is a constant source of solace toward an ache that never goes away.

I see him reading Isaac Asimov or H.G. Wells or even Tolstoy eventually. In fact, I have already sent him THE DEATH OF IVAN ILYICH. I may even get him to read Chaucer before he's executed by lethal injection.

This educating, this hopeful literary therapy on my part, is all part of my own healing process over my father's murder forty-five years ago. Troy's acquaintance has assuaged a desperate need I have to understand how someone could kill my father in cold blood.

I, too, have gotten angry, but not to the point of beating people to death with a baseball bat, which is what Troy and his friends did to the kids in Deltona, Florida. Not to the point of pointing a shotgun at someone's face through a kitchen window and pulling the trigger,

which is what happened to my father in his Winter Park suburban home.

I understand that Troy is what his lawyers called "a poster child" for a death row inmate. In a way he was groomed for that destiny all his life by a tragic series of unwholesome events. He is not a genius, but he is not stupid by any means. I've met his mother, and I know she loves him. Under different circumstances, his life could have turned out a lot better, maybe even well. Instead, he is on death row, and he is not likely to leave except on a gurney. My father is dead and his killer roams free. There is so much injustice in the world and the only thing I can do about it is try to forgive.

Troy is an experiment in forgiveness on my part. My father was instrumental in my love for literature, and that passion has influenced my life. I am now extending that lifeline, that good influence, to a convicted killer.

I think about these things during my daily walk, which takes up an hour. When I walk, if it is late enough, I see worms writhing on the sidewalks, frying in the Florida heat. I always make a point to pick them up and place them in the grass. I see a lot of roadkill too—carcasses and bones of armadillos, a bird, a raccoon freshly killed on the side of the road, haunting me because he was young and curled up as though he were sleeping.

It is easy for me to empathize with these disparate forms of life, perhaps too easy. I have often felt powerless, threatened, overwhelmed by forces I don't understand. Just the act of my walking the earth is an affront to creatures who have gone before me, whose homes and lives were ruthlessly demolished to make way for beings bigger and better equipped for destruction.

So I put the worms and cicadas back in the grass and say a prayer for dead wildlife rotting on the side of the road. Sometimes I feel despair that is beyond healing, beyond forgiveness.

Sometimes, though, I feel hope that there is much to be done for the world. Sometimes I care a lot about the good I still need to do. Doing good assuages, even a little bit, the essential wrongness of the world. It is a constant source of solace toward an ache that never goes away.

It would be a good thing for Troy to admit what he's done and to ask for forgiveness. That is unrealistic, however, and likely will never happen. But maybe he's done a little good by helping me to understand that even a mass murderer, the lowest of the low, is a living being created by God. And maybe I've done him a little good by giving him different perspectives through literature.

There is an affirmation from *THE COURSE IN MIRACLES* that I say to myself every single day: *Only my condemnation injures me, only my forgiveness sets me free.*

My correspondence with a convicted murderer is how I forgive my father's unknown killer. It's not a perfect solution, but it's all I've got. ◆

The liberation of Saint Peter. Raphael, 1513-1514. Wall fresco, the Vatican, Rome

A former Jain monk, now a renowned editor and activist, considers....

Jains celebrating the Das Lakshana (Paryusana) festival of forgiveness and introspection. Jain Center of America, Flushing, New York, 2012. Photograph by Aayush18

The Power of Forgiveness

Satish Kumar

*It's one of the greatest gifts you can give yourself, to forgive.
Forgive everybody.*
Maya Angelou

To LIVE SIMPLY and practice spiritual simplicity, I had to acquire the power of forgiveness. During my eight thousand mile walk [for peace—the eds.] across the continents, I faced a gun twice. Once in Paris and a second time in Atlanta, Georgia, in the United States. In Paris I was mistaken by a white Frenchman with a gun for an Algerian terrorist. This was at the time when the Algerian war was coming to an end, and he thought I might be dangerous. It was ironic. I had just walked all the way from India to Paris via Moscow, promoting peace, nonviolence, and forgiveness, and here I was in the heart of civilization being misidentified as someone violent, maybe a terrorist.

I escaped death thanks to a friend whom I was visiting. She explained to the gunman that I was no terrorist, I was her friend, I was a peacemaker. Afterwards she wanted to report my assailant to the police, but I said, "The man who was carrying the gun is full of fear. He is afraid of losing something, perhaps his superiority as a white man, perhaps his life itself, or some other fear. In the end he has to come to terms with his fear and overcome it. This cannot be done by locking him up."

My host said, "But you might have been killed!"

I replied, "Yes, I might have, but one can only die once. One can live a long life full of fear and revenge. I do not wish to live like that."

The second story is similar. In 1964, after meeting Martin Luther King in Atlanta, Georgia, an English friend invited me to a restaurant not knowing that it was for whites only. The waiters refused to serve us, so I went up to see the manager to ask for an explanation. He said, "We don't do explanations, leave immediately, no ifs, no buts."

I replied, "No I am not leaving." By now I realized that the cause for the refusal was the color of my skin.

"Get out!" he shouted at me. Waiters and customers gathered around.

I said, "I am sorry, but why are you angry? I have done no harm to you. I am only asking for a cup of tea. We can pay for it in advance. Is there any problem?"

The manager opened a drawer, pulled out a gun, and said, "Get out immediately or…" By now many more people had gathered, and they and the waiters took hold of me and pushed me out the door.

Later I complained about the incident to the State Department because I thought the U.S. government needs to know what is going on in the restaurants of their country. My intention was not to seek punishment for the restaurateur but, hopefully, to change the law. I received an apology from the State Department. But in any case, I felt no bitterness. The proprietor was acting out of fear, the fear of losing white superiority, the fear of being overwhelmed by the power of the black minority. Martin Luther King stated that the white community did not need to fear the black. The black community did not wish to rule over the white, but neither did they wish to be ruled by them. We are all equal in the eyes of God. Whatever color we are, we all have red blood under our skin. Basic human dignity and the dignity of life is the prerogative of us all.

I have learned that the art of forgiveness can go hand in hand with the art of acting for a just cause. Forgiveness does not mean surrender to injustice, and acting for justice does not mean taking revenge or inflicting injury upon your opponent.

For me, the practice of forgiveness goes back to my Jain roots. As a child monk until the age of eighteen, every night before going to bed I would chant a mantra of forgiveness:

I forgive all living beings upon this earth.

I beg forgiveness from all living beings.

I cherish friendship with all living beings.

I have no enemies.

If I lay down having forgotten to say this prayer, I would get up, close my eyes, be still, and chant the mantra twice. It was not just a case of uttering the words. I would feel the meaning deeply, along with a profound sense of my unity with all life. "The idea that anyone can be your enemy is false," said my guru. "You make an enemy of the other only through your fear, so your fear is your enemy. Conquer fear and you have conquered all enemies."

In addition to this daily practice, Jains have an annual festival of forgiveness. During the monsoon season, there is a day when all Jains fast for twenty-four hours. I consumed nothing but boiled water and spent all my waking hours remembering thoughts, words, or actions which may have been harsh or harmful and which may have caused hurt to someone during the year. This was a time of sincere and genuine

Freedom from fear is the fruit of forgiveness. When we are free from fear, we can create conditions conducive to the creativity which is absolutely necessary for human well-being.

reflection. I repeated the words "I forgive, I forgive, I forgive" after each recollection of anger, irritation, or arrogance. As I sought forgiveness from others, I also forgave myself for my shortcomings.

I remember vividly that after twenty-four hours of physical and mental detoxification, I felt light and healed, as if a huge burden had been taken from my shoulders. After breaking my fast, I went to my friends and family members and asked for forgiveness face to face. I bowed down and touched the feet of my fellow monks and told them in all sincerity that I harbored no ill feeling or sense of hurt even if they had annoyed me. I came to seek forgiveness and also to give forgiveness.

On this day, Jains also write letters asking for forgiveness and giving forgiveness if their friends and family are not near enough for them to do so in person. Forgiving yourself, forgiving your fellow human beings, and seeking forgiveness from others creates the ground on which compassion, generosity, mutuality, reciprocity, communication, and love can grow. There cannot be a sense of harmony and peace without forgiveness.

Freedom from fear is the fruit of forgiveness. When we are free from fear, we can create conditions conducive to the creativity which is absolutely necessary for human well-being. When

we are boiling with rage and the desire for revenge, we are incapable of finding physical, mental, or spiritual fulfillment. Happiness is a consequence of a calm mind. According to Jains, the purpose of life is to find happiness or *ananda*. Happiness occurs when we make no enemies, when we have no enemies, when we give no offense and take no offense. If someone tries to be an enemy, we can often dissolve their animosity through patience and forgiveness.

Forgiveness is only possible when someone has hurt us, wounded us, or insulted us. Such negative acts offer us an opportunity to cultivate and manifest compassion which is the antidote to revenge. If no one acted negatively or harmfully, then there would be no opportunity to practice forgiveness. If someone hurts us and we hurt them back, then we descend to their level. Their violence plus our violence doubles the amount of violence. An increase of aggression helps no one. One cannot extinguish a fire by putting on more fuel. The only way to put out the fire of aggression and anger is with the water of forgiveness. The water of forgiveness is not merely a passive process of not reacting negatively. The water of forgiveness is a positive action to see good in an individual even when you are faced with extreme negativity.

Vinoba Bhave [1895–1982, considered by many the spiritual heir to Gandhi—the eds.] used to explain the royal road to forgiveness to us. There are some skeptics who can only see faults in everyone. Their skepticism prevents them from practicing forgiveness. Then there are people who see some good and some bad in everyone; these are the rationalists. For them, practicing forgiveness is also difficult. Then there are people who mainly see good in everyone. They can begin to practice forgiveness. Then there are those who, on finding some small virtue in others, magnify it, praise it extravagantly, and shower them with appreciation. These are the people on the royal road to forgiveness.

I questioned whether this kind of behavior was honest and truthful. Vinoba responded that when you see a small virtue in someone, you need to realize that this good quality represents a reservoir of virtue hidden in their hearts. By focusing on that virtue, you shine a light on it. It is comparable to reading a map in which one inch represents ten miles. Although on the map you see an inch, you know that on the ground it is ten miles. In the same way, you may look at one small virtue in a badly behaved person and know that he or she has the potential to be a saint. In fact, it is possible to transform an evil person into a saint by forgiveness.

Vinoba himself had great generosity of spirit. No wonder he was able to inspire and persuade landlords, often thought to be mean and greedy, to donate land and share their wealth with the landless poor. It was a miracle that Vinoba collected 4.5 million acres of land in gifts which were distributed among the lowest of the low, laborers who possessed nothing.

At public meetings, in Vinoba's presence, landlords asked for forgiveness from the poor who their families had exploited for generations. In return the landless laborers offered forgiveness to the landlords under whose regime they and their ancestors had suffered. The exchange of forgiveness healed the wounds of lifetimes. At last, in many villages there was reconciliation and peace.

Another example in Vinoba's life was the surrender of bandits and dacoits (armed robbers) who were ravaging and pillaging the rural population of central India. This came about because Vinoba dared to go to them with love and the force of forgiveness. He spoke to them with respect. "You are rebels, I too am a rebel, the only difference between us is that I use the weapon of compassion. But I praise you for your spirit of rebellion and courage, let us join together to bring justice and equality to our society." Until then everybody had condemned these people and called them criminals, but Vinoba called them rebels, men of courage. His words brought about a change of heart, and these armed rebels surrendered their weapons, seeking and giving forgiveness. They had to undergo the legal process and received a period of imprisonment, but they gained a new respect and praise from the public, the press, and the government. Eventually they and their families were rehabilitated by being given land to farm and capital to start cottage industries....

Another wonderful example of forgiveness is Jo Berry. She is the daughter of Sir Anthony

Mahatma Gandhi (l.) and Vinoba Bhave (r.)

Berry, a Conservative Member of Parliament who was killed by the Irish Republican Army (IRA) in the Brighton hotel bombing in 1984, while attending the annual Conservative Party conference. Jo said to me that the trauma and grief of losing her father in such a shocking way made her think long and hard. "I can seek revenge or I can seek peace," she thought. She chose forgiveness in place of blame and hatred.

"The hardest bridge to build was with Patrick Magee, who planted the bomb which killed my father," she remembered. "After he was released from prison, I met him at a friend's house in Dublin. I was scared. At first he defended his political perspective, but then he started to hear my pain. Something changed. He had taken off his political hat, and his human heart opened. I said to him, 'Let us forgive each other. Whatever I do, nothing will bring my father back, but let us do something together so that no daughter or son loses their father in such violent circumstances in the future.'"

This was a true moment of reconciliation. Jo Berry, a victim of violence, forgave Patrick Magee, perpetrator of her father's death. From then on, they have worked together to build bridges for peace. They have spoken together at more than a hundred meetings, reaching people with their inspiring narrative. They remind their audiences that violence begets violence, revenge begets revenge. The only way forward is to forgive and forget and begin anew. As the saying goes:

The first to apologize is the bravest.

The first to forgive is the strongest.

The first to forget is the happiest.

How long can we carry the burden of the past? History is full of atrocities and cruelties, slavery, racism, colonialism, apartheid, the Holocaust, and genocide in one form or another.

Patrick Magee had been given eight life sentences. The judge branded him as a man of exceptional cruelty and inhumanity. In the end he served fourteen years in prison and was released as part of the Good Friday agreement which brought an end to sectarian strife in Ireland. Now he is a transformed man devoting his entire life to planting the seeds of love in place of hate. It is said, "There is no love without forgiveness, and there is no forgiveness without love." This story shows that good and bad runs through every human heart, and that every human being has the potential to be transformed. The power of compassion and forgiveness is greater than the power of punishment and revenge....

From my personal experience as well as the experience of socially and politically active campaigners, I have found ample evidence of resolving conflict through forgiveness, whereas revenge and punishment only exacerbate wounds and divisions and bring no healing. We have had enough of conflicts and wars. Now is the time for the people of the world to commit themselves to the way of negotiation. Negotiation and forgiveness is the way of the brave and courageous. As Mahatma Gandhi said, "The weak can never forgive, forgiveness is an attribute of the strong."

There have been many examples of conflicts and forgiveness within the context of human societies. Today the overwhelming conflict is between human greed and Earth's capacity. During the past few centuries, industrial societies have ravaged the Earth's resources, treating animals, forests, and oceans as mines from which to extract wealth. It seems that humanity is at war with Nature. We treat the land and pollute the biosphere as if we were at war. The mission of modern society appears to be to conquer Nature.

A time will come when humanity recognizes its folly and asks for forgiveness from the Earth. As yet, the majority of people have not recognized their stupidity and recklessness. They still believe it is their prerogative to use the natural world to meet the increasing demands of the worldwide consumer society. Although a growing minority of people around the world recognize that humans need to live simply within the limits of the finite Earth and consider themselves an integral part of Nature rather than her master, this view is still not mainstream. It may be some time before we realize this grave mistake. But sooner or later, the time will come when we need to ask for the Earth's forgiveness. I believe the Earth is bountiful and generous enough to forgive us, and we may be able to repair the damage we have caused. But if we don't realize our mistakes in time, then sadly but surely human survival will be in danger.

Increasingly, many people recognize that humanity has to live in harmony with the Earth. At the end of 2015, nearly two hundred world governments gathered together and unanimously agreed that due to human activities and particularly the excessive use of fossil fuels, the climate is changing, and this change will have a catastrophic impact on planet Earth and on the survival of human civilization as well as many species. Surprisingly, most world governments are now in the process of ratifying the Paris Agreement.

If these governments stay true to their commitment and implement the policy of reducing their carbon emissions, that will be, in my view, a step towards asking forgiveness of the Earth.

On a nongovernmental level, many communities are taking actions to mitigate the damage human activities have inflicted upon the Earth. The Transition Town movement is an inspiring example of people taking responsibility for making the transition from a fossil fuel based lifestyle to one based on renewable energy. The Transition movement claims to include nearly four hundred towns and communities around the world taking initiatives to moderate their dependence on exploitative and harmful systems. In Devon, where I live, Tornes was the first such town, and I have witnessed a change not only of attitudes but also of lifestyles in a way which establishes a more humble and grateful relationship with our planet home. This humility is in itself a way of asking forgiveness from the Earth.

Right relationship, radical love, and unconditional forgiveness are the fruits of a deep conviction that life is full of paradoxes, dilemmas, and choices pulling us in opposing directions. In such situations, we have to rise above the dialectics of opposites and reach out for a state of equilibrium through the practice of equanimity. By doing so, we will be better equipped to live a life of elegant simplicity. ◆

Reprinted by permission (abridged) from Satish Kumar's *ELEGANT SIMPLICITY: THE ART OF LIVING WELL* (New Society Publishers, www.newsociety.com, 2019)

Blue Marble, Eastern Hemisphere. NASA images by Reto Stöckli

By the Mill Pond. Hans Gude, 1850. Oil on paper. National Gallery of Norway, Oslo

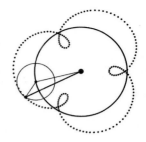

The Woman Without a Shadow

Anonymous / Scandinavian Folk Tale

Collected by Svend Grundtvig. Retold by Betsy Cornwell

ONCE THERE WAS A WOMAN who was afraid of having children. All the other women she knew were afraid of *not* having them, so she felt alone in her fear; and that made her even more afraid. Her new husband, the town pastor, wanted children very much. She wished to change her own mind in order to please him, but she could not.

The woman's fear grew deeper the longer she was married. Other women spoke of help they had received from a wise woman who lived in the forest—a woman her husband called a wicked witch—and she wondered if this wise woman could help her, too.

So one night, after her husband fell asleep, the woman left her marriage bed and walked into the woods. She came to the wise woman's cottage, which was overgrown with flowering vines so that she could barely see it. She brushed the vines aside and knocked on the cottage's wooden door.

An ancient crone opened it and gestured for her to come in.

The younger woman sat at the table inside and explained her fear. The crone listened, and then she got up and looked through her shelves and cupboards. She picked up a small wicker basket containing seven white stones and set it down before the younger woman.

"Throw these seven stones into a well that you will pass as you return home, and you will be protected from bearing children," she said.

The woman thanked the crone and, leaving behind a coin she had taken from her husband's full coffer as payment, she left the cottage and began her walk back through the forest.

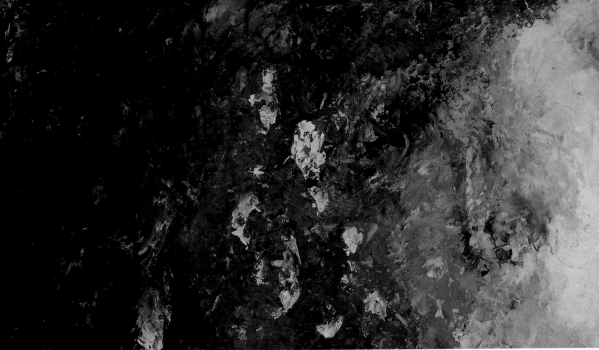

Wonderland. August Strindberg, 1894. Oil on paperboard. Nationalmuseum, Stockholm

Soon she came to a well, just as the crone had said she would. She looked down into it, but the well was so deep that she could see only darkness inside, in spite of the full moon above her.

She threw the stones one by one into the well. With every splash, she thought she heard the cry of a child.

As the last stone left her hand, something thin and dark slipped from behind her and followed the stone down into the water. The woman felt suddenly lighter, as if a weight had lifted from her body.

She went home and got back into bed, where she fell quickly and peacefully asleep.

A month later, the woman attended an evening funeral over which her husband presided. After the funeral, they left the church together.

As they walked through the churchyard under the light of the full moon, her husband noticed that the woman cast no shadow.

"Wife!" he cried. "What monstrous sin have you committed, that God has seen fit to take your shadow away?"

The woman said she did not know, but her husband pressed her and threatened her until she finally admitted what she had done.

"Please forgive me," she said. "I did this because I am afraid to have children."

"Cursed woman!" her husband replied, shaking with anger. "Forgive you? Not even God could forgive such an unnatural fear, or such an act of dark magic. Flowers will grow from my fine house's slate roof before God forgives a woman like you." The pastor pointed down the road that led away from the churchyard, away from their town. "Leave this holy ground. You are no wife for me nor for any man. I never wish to see you again."

So the woman turned away from the pastor and set off down the road. Moonlight shone through her body as if she was made of glass.

Many years passed. The pastor wished to marry again, but all the women in town had seen his unkindness to his first wife, and he was unable to persuade any of them to take him as a husband. He hired a housekeeper to cook and clean for him, and he advanced into a bitter and resentful old age.

One night, as the pastor was out preaching at evening service, his housekeeper heard a knock on the door. She opened it and saw an elderly woman wrapped in a traveling cloak.

"I must beg your hospitality," the woman said. "I have been traveling for many years, and I find I have nowhere to lay my head tonight."

The housekeeper welcomed the woman inside and fed her a good dinner, then settled her beside the fire with a hot drink. The old woman fell asleep before the fire, and when the housekeeper collected her cup she saw that the woman cast no shadow; but she thought it was the woman's own business, and none of hers, and she went up to bed.

The pastor came home late, and he went straight to bed too, without noticing the old woman who slept before the fire in his living room.

The housekeeper rose early the next morning and saw the old woman slumped in her chair. Thinking she slept, the housekeeper began her morning tasks.

When the pastor came downstairs some time later, he saw the woman and gasped with rage. Even after all the years that had passed, he recognized her at once.

He rushed over and began to shake her, but she would not rouse; her body was cold, and her face unchanging and serene. He soon realized that she was dead.

"Pastor!" he heard his housekeeper cry from outside, where she was sweeping the front steps. "Come and see! You will not believe it!"

The pastor hurried outside. The housekeeper pointed up at the slate roof of his fine house. It was blooming all over with flowers. ◆

Photograph by Jay Wennington

A Buddhist priest's recipe for what ails you

Bamboo: Or, How to Turn Poison into a Meal

Gesshin Claire Greenwood

IF THERE IS A BETTER METAPHOR for Buddhist practice than turning inedible vegetables into delicious food, I cannot think of it. In Buddhist practice and in the kitchen, our goal should always be to meet adverse and unpleasant circumstances skillfully, transforming them into something workable and useful. Much of monastery life is spent caring for and treating vegetables for this very reason.

Usually we think of monasteries as sullen, isolated places, filled with monks intent on renouncing the world. This is partially true, as renunciation is a foundational value of monasticism. But monasteries are an integral part of the fabric of society in Asia; they are surrounded by people, seasons, governments, farms, and festivals. Monks tend to the physical and spiritual well-being of their parishioners and are responsible for ushering dead spirits safely into the afterlife. In return, devout laypeople donate food, time, or money—a portion of their yearly rice crop, their best homemade pickles, or leftovers from their shops.

As when dealing with bamboo, we learn that transforming emotional poison takes bravery, patience, and, in the beginning, guidance.

Food donations in particular match the vicissitudes of the seasons. In Japan, since people donated what they grew themselves, we would receive a large number of cabbages and radishes in the winter, plums and bamboo sprouts in the spring, tomatoes and cucumbers in the summer, and mushrooms in the fall. Although of course we appreciated these donations, sometimes we would have only one kind of vegetable to eat. For example, there would be more cucumbers than we could possibly eat, but only cucumbers.

A togan is a Japanese melon with a hard texture that is considered a delicacy and is usually only found in specialty restaurants. However, some winters we would receive dozens and dozens of togan. I remember the basement being filled with small mountains of them. We would eat them for breakfast, lunch, and dinner, served all kinds of ways: cooked and then simmered in soy broth, covered with a thickened Chinese sauce, or sliced thin in salads. There was no throwing these vegetables out or giving them away.

Working for years in Japanese kitchens as I did, I came to learn that many Japanese vegetables, especially those considered delicacies, are poisonous or inedible in their natural state. Umeboshi, or pickled plums, are made from small plums that are inedible until pickled in salt. I have spent countless hours over a sink peeling off the celery-like skin of fuki, or butterbur,

which stains your fingers brown. Mountain yams need to be peeled before grating, but the white inside is a skin irritant, so there is a special way to grate the yam without allowing the white part to touch your hands.

Of all the poisonous, inedible, hand-staining, and hand-irritating vegetables I have cooked with, there is a special place in my heart for *takenoko*, or bamboo. In Japan, bamboo shoots are literally weeds; they appear overnight in April and May like crop circles (and sometimes in circles!), and if they are left to proliferate, they will take over entire mountains. They grow at an alarming rate, often doubling in height overnight. Thus, for a few weeks in the spring, people in the countryside spend their days chopping down baby bamboo and then serving up Bamboo Rice or Clear Soup with Bamboo Shoots and Wakame.

Despite its delicate, almost nonexistent flavor, bamboo is a dangerous vegetable. Untreated, bamboo is inedible, and even if it is prepared correctly, eating too much bamboo can make people break out in hives. There is a certain ridiculousness to bamboo as well. It has brown, hairy bark that makes it look like an elephant's trunk before you take the bark off in sheets. I've seen bamboo shoots as small as an asparagus stalk and as large as a small dog.

Bamboo can be transformed from an inedible tree into a delicacy worthy of inclusion in soup, stir-fries, stews, or rice by cooking the bamboo trunk in leftover rice water (or water with rice bran added) over low heat for a couple of hours. Using rice water will remove toxins and make the bamboo less bitter. When the bamboo is cool, the brown bark can be peeled off (using rubber gloves, as the bark can irritate hands) to reveal the white center.

Different parts of the bamboo trunk are used for different dishes. The very bottom of the bamboo, ringed by a layer of eerie black bumps, is hard and almost inedible; it is basically a tree. After the black bumps are cut off, the hard flesh underneath can be ground in a food processor, mixed with cornstarch, and made into dumplings. The middle section, also hard, is sliced thin, so that it can be cooked thoroughly in a stir-fry, such as Chinese-style chop-suey, or fried with hot pepper, soy sauce, and sugar. The pointy top part of the bamboo is the softest and most delicious part. If it is very young, it can be eaten without further cooking, with just wasabi and soy sauce. More commonly, though, this soft bamboo shows up in soups or is lightly simmered in soy broth and then arranged with other vegetables such as carrots, shiitake mushrooms, and green beans.

Bamboo is a challenging vegetable. Most Japanese people these days (and Americans who wish to cook with it) buy it preboiled and peeled at the supermarket. But I think this takes the magic out of the whole spring bamboo explosion. There is a certain fun in the immensity of treating bamboo and cooking it yourself—being up to your elbows in hairy bamboo bark and rice bran-colored water. And what is better for Zen practice than converting a giant elephant tusk-like, semipoisonous weed into food?

Many experiences in life seem like unpeeled bamboo—inedible, ridiculous, ugly, and hard. Maybe we hate our job, are struggling in school, or find that our best friend is starting to get on our nerves. And maybe, like an unskilled farmer, we think the easiest thing is to throw these experiences away—quit our job, change majors, change friends. But a good cook knows how to turn even the most terrifying, skin-irritating vegetable into a delicacy.

The more experience we have transforming poison into a meal, the more comfortable we become with difficult conversations, with immense tasks, with facing the unknown. As when dealing with bamboo, we learn that transforming emotional poison takes bravery, patience, and, in the beginning, guidance. But once we are used to it, it becomes natural. We come to respect and understand our life's strange vegetables—the difficult friends, the unsatisfying careers. We learn to attend to them with attention and energy. We know which ingredients to mix in. It is a step-by-step process. It takes time, but it is not in and of itself difficult. First put the bamboo into a pot. Then add rice bran and water. The difficulty is in renewing our intention, in not giving up. In this way, we can transform any poison into a meal.

If you have finished detoxifying your bamboo—or if you have bought it preboiled and peeled from a store — the first dish you will want to make will be Bamboo Rice.

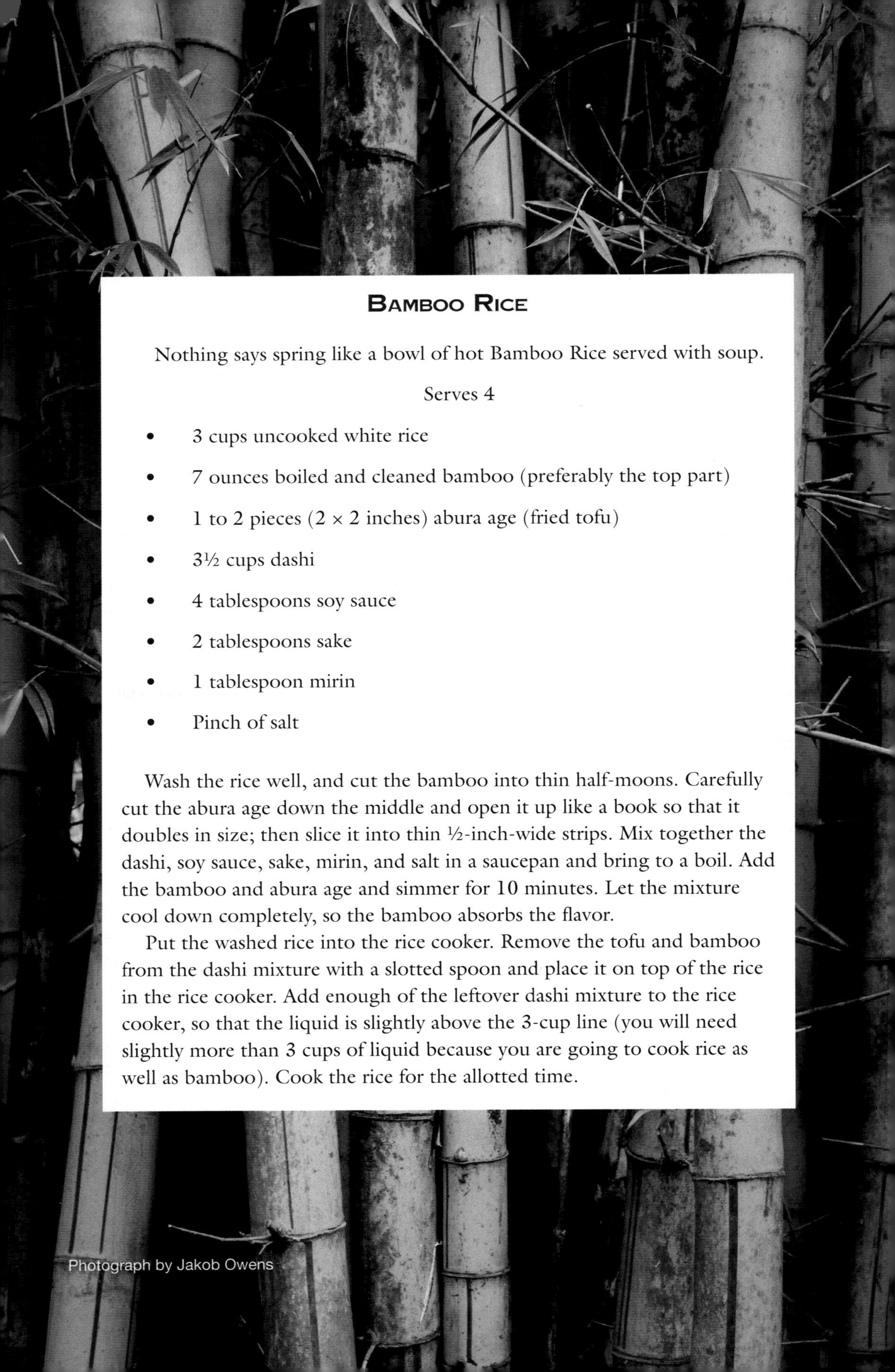

BAMBOO RICE

Nothing says spring like a bowl of hot Bamboo Rice served with soup.

Serves 4

- 3 cups uncooked white rice

- 7 ounces boiled and cleaned bamboo (preferably the top part)

- 1 to 2 pieces (2 × 2 inches) abura age (fried tofu)

- 3½ cups dashi

- 4 tablespoons soy sauce

- 2 tablespoons sake

- 1 tablespoon mirin

- Pinch of salt

Wash the rice well, and cut the bamboo into thin half-moons. Carefully cut the abura age down the middle and open it up like a book so that it doubles in size; then slice it into thin ½-inch-wide strips. Mix together the dashi, soy sauce, sake, mirin, and salt in a saucepan and bring to a boil. Add the bamboo and abura age and simmer for 10 minutes. Let the mixture cool down completely, so the bamboo absorbs the flavor.

Put the washed rice into the rice cooker. Remove the tofu and bamboo from the dashi mixture with a slotted spoon and place it on top of the rice in the rice cooker. Add enough of the leftover dashi mixture to the rice cooker, so that the liquid is slightly above the 3-cup line (you will need slightly more than 3 cups of liquid because you are going to cook rice as well as bamboo). Cook the rice for the allotted time.

Cooked giant timber bamboo sprouts, 2006. Photograph by Pdeitiker

There is a certain spiritual (and olfactory) satisfaction in transforming a poisonous weed into a meal. And yet no matter how skillful we are as cooks, the body knows bamboo is not to be eaten every day. It is still, fundamentally, a dangerous plant. One year at the monastery when we had an influx of bamboo, the kitchen served it several times a day. Eventually, people started getting sick.

Just as we can pay attention to having just enough money, food, or material objects, it is useful to become aware of when there is too much toxicity in our lives. A little bit of bamboo is wonderful once in a while, but eating it every day can make our skin break out in hives or cause indigestion. Similarly, it's useful to know when the pain of a relationship or the strain of a physical sensation is too much. Sitting in meditation is good, but it's possible to sit for too long and injure ourselves physically. We need to be tuned in to how our body relates to pain and difficulty.

Personally, I have discovered that when I sit for a long time in one position, my body feels cramped and achy. In meditation, if those feelings are due to restlessness, it's useful to sit through them. But there is a different kind of pain, the pain of injuring the body, that also appears when we sit for long periods of time. It is crucial to understand the difference. Sitting through boredom is useful; enduring injury is not.

Some difficult relationships and experiences can be treated like bamboo. We can boil them and transform the poison into a delicacy. This is powerful emotional alchemy. But other relationships will always be toxic. They will grow worse over time, and we only hurt ourselves and others by trying to fix them. It's important to leave this kind of poison behind. The more we pay attention to our bodies and listen deeply, the more we can understand which pain or poison is detrimental and which kind can be useful. ◆

WELCOME TO THE
PARABOLA
BACK ISSUE LIBRARY

CHOOSE FROM OVER 160 BACK ISSUES TO INFORM, INSPIRE, AND GUIDE YOU ON YOUR JOURNEY.

All Back Issues listed as in print below are $12.50 plus shipping and handling.

All Back Issues listed in green below are out-of-print but are available here as Parabola Archived paper editions at $20.00 each plus shipping and handling, or as electronic files for $7.50 each at www.parabola.org.

1:1 THE HERO In quest of the meaning of Self
1:2 MAGIC The power that transforms
1:3 INITIATION A portal to rebirth
1:4 RITES OF PASSAGE Symbols and rituals of transformation

2:1 DEATH Beyond the limits of the known
2:2 CREATION From formlessness, something new
2:3 COSMOLOGY The order of things, seen and unseen
2:4 RELATIONSHIPS Our interwoven human experience

3:1 SACRED SPACE Landscapes, temples, the inner terrain
3:2 SACRIFICE & TRANSFORMATION Stepping into a holy fire
3:3 INNER ALCHEMY Refining the gold within
3:4 ANDROGYNY The fusion of male and female

4:1 THE TRICKSTER Guide, mischief-maker, master of disguise
4:2 SACRED DANCE Moving to worship, moving to transcend
4:3 THE CHILD Setting out from innocence
4:4 STORYTELLING & EDUCATION Speaking to young minds

5:1 THE OLD ONES Visions of our elders
5:2 MUSIC, SOUND, & SILENCE Echoes of stillness
5:3 OBSTACLES In the way, or the Way itself?
5:4 WOMAN In search of the feminine

6:1 EARTH & SPIRIT Opposites or complements?
6:2 THE DREAM OF PROGRESS Our modern fantasy
6:3 MASK & METAPHOR When things are not as they seem
6:4 DEMONS Spirits of the dark

7:1 SLEEP To be restored, or to forget
7:2 DREAMS & SEEING Visions, fantasy, and the unconscious
7:3 CEREMONIES Seeking divine service
7:4 HOLY WAR Conflict for the sake of reconciliation

8:1 GUILT The burden of conscience
8:2 ANIMALS The nature of the creature world
8:3 WORDS OF POWER Secret words, magic spells, divine utterances
8:4 SUN & MOON Partners in time as fields of force

9:1 HIERARCHY The ladder of the sacred
9:2 THEFT The paradox of possession
9:3 PILGRIMAGE Journey toward the holy
9:4 FOOD Nourishing body and spirit

10:1 WHOLENESS The hunger for completion
10:2 EXILE Cut off from the homeland of meaning
10:3 THE BODY Half dust, half deity
10:4 THE SEVEN DEADLY SINS The mystery of goodness

11:1 THE WITNESS Silent guides and unsleeping eyes
11:2 MIRRORS That which reflects the real
11:3 SADNESS The transformation of tragedy
11:4 MEMORY & FORGETTING What we remember and why

12:1 THE KNIGHT & THE HERMIT Heroes of action and reflection
12:2 ADDICTION The prison of human craving
12:3 FORGIVENESS The past transcended
12:4 THE SENSE OF HUMOR Walking with laughter

13:1 THE CREATIVE RESPONSE To represent the sacred
13:2 REPETITION & RENEWAL Respecting the rhythm of growth
13:3 QUESTIONS The road to understanding
13:4 THE MOUNTAIN A meeting place of Earth and Heaven

14:1 DISCIPLES & DISCIPLINE Teachers, masters, students, fools
14:2 TRADITION & TRANSMISSION Passages from wisdom into wisdom
14:3 THE TREE OF LIFE Root, trunk, and crown of our search
14:4 TRIAD Sacred and secular laws of three

15:1 TIME & PRESENCE How to welcome the present moment
15:2 ATTENTION What animates mind, body, and feeling
15:3 LIBERATION Freedom from what, freedom for what?
15:4 HOSPITALITY Care in human relationships

16:1 MONEY Exchange between humans, and with the divine
16:2 THE HUNTER Stalking great knowledge
16:3 CRAFT The skill that leads to creation
16:4 THE GOLDEN MEAN Balance between defect and excess

17:1 SOLITUDE & COMMUNITY The self, alone and with others
17:2 LABYRINTH The path to inner treasure
17:3 THE ORAL TRADITION Transmission by spoken word and silence
17:4 POWER & ENERGY The stunning array of atom and cosmos

18:1 HEALING The return to a state of health
18:2 PLACE & SPACE Seeking the holy in mountain, sea, and vale
18:3 CROSSROADS The meeting place of traditions and ideas
18:4 THE CITY Hub of the human world

19:1 THE CALL To ask for help, to receive what is given
19:2 TWINS The two who come from one
19:3 CLOTHING Concealing and revealing our inner selves
19:4 HIDDEN TREASURE Value, hope, and knowledge

20:1 EARTH, AIR, WATER, FIRE Essential elements of all things
20:2 THE STRANGER Messenger or deceiver, savior or threat
20:3 LANGUAGE & MEANING Communication, symbol, and sign
20:4 EROS Human sexuality and the life of the spirit

21:1 PROPHETS & PROPHECY Seeing beyond the veil
21:2 THE SOUL Life within and beyond our corporeal existence
21:3 PEACE Seeking inner and outer tranquility
21:4 PLAY & WORK Struggle and release in the search for meaning

22:1 WAYS OF KNOWING Different avenues to truth
22:2 THE SHADOW Cast by the light we follow
22:3 CONSCIENCE & CONSCIOUSNESS Inner guides to understanding one's being
22:4 MIRACLES Enigmatic breaks in the laws of nature

23:1 MILLENNIUM To what end, to what beginning?
23:2 ECSTASY Joy that transports us outside of ourselves
23:3 FEAR Sign of weakness, or of strength?
23:4 BIRTH AND REBIRTH Journey toward renewal

24:1 NATURE Exploring inner and outer terrain
24:2 PRAYER & MEDITATION Petition, praise, gratitude, confession
24:3 NUMBER & SYMBOL Languages that disclose the real
24:4 EVIL The duality within us, within the world

25:1 **THRESHOLD** Neither here nor there, real nor imaginary
25:2 **RIDDLE & MYSTERY** Questions and answers
25:3 **THE TEACHER** One who shows the way
25:4 **FATE AND FORTUNE** Inevitabilities that speak to us

26:1 **THE GARDEN** Cultivating within and without
26:2 **LIGHT** That which illuminates our inner and outer darkness
26:3 **THE FOOL** In search of divine innocence
26:4 **THE HEART** Where the quest begins and ends

27:1 **THE EGO AND THE "I"** Which one is real?
27:2 **DYING** Ending or beginning of transformation?
27:3 **GRACE** Gifts bestowed from above
27:4 **WAR** Violence as a means to an end

28:1 **COMPASSION** Actions that embrace others
28:2 **PRISON** Inner and outer confinement
28:3 **CHAOS AND ORDER** The interplay of creative forces
28:4 **TRUTH AND ILLUSION** Seeking clarity amidst   confusion

29:1 **MARRIAGE** Union with the Other
29:2 **WEB OF LIFE** The interrelationship of being
29:3 **THE SEEKER** In search of the Way
29:4 **FRIENDSHIP** Companions on the path

30:1 **AWAKENING** Casting off slumber
30:2 **RESTRAINT** The power of not doing
30:3 **BODY AND SOUL** Two mysteries
30:4 **FUNDAMENTALISM** Getting out of the box

31:1 **COMING TO OUR SENSES** Shaking our senses free
31:2 **ABSENCE AND LONGING** The path of yearning
31:3 **THINKING** Thinking as prayer
31:4 **HOME** The homes of great spiritual leaders

32:1 **FAITH** Seven great acts of faith
32:2 **SEX** Spiritual teachings on sex
32:3 **HOLY EARTH** Our sacred planet
32:4 **THE NEW WORLD** Frontiers of the spiritual

33:1 **SILENCE** The place of not speaking
33:2 **GOD** Approaching the Unknown
33:3 **MAN & MACHINE** Traditions & technology
33:4 **JUSTICE** The Divine measure

34:1 **IMAGINATION** The story issue
34:2 **WATER** The sacred element
34:3 **THE PATH** Finding the right way
34:4 **THE FUTURE** The way ahead

35:1 **LOVE** The divine energy
35:2 **LIFE AFTER DEATH** Beyond the known
35:3 **DESIRE** What compels our lives?
35:4 **BEAUTY** What transports us; where do we look?

36:1 **SUFFERING** To be with it, and to let it be
36:2 **GIVING & RECEIVING** Gift of life, flow of mediating energies
36:3 **SEEING** An act of attentiveness in body, mind, and heart
36:4 **MANY PATHS ONE TRUTH** Finding the light, within and without

37:1 **BURNING WORLD** Healing a world in crisis
37:2 **ALONE & TOGETHER** Balancing solitude and community
37:3 **THE UNKNOWN** We, ourselves, are the deepest unknown
37:4 **SCIENCE & SPIRIT** How both serve to apprehend Reality

38:1 **SPIRIT IN THE WORLD** Reflections on embodiment
38:2 **HEAVEN & HELL** Symbolic and timeless, real and present
38:3 **POWER** Ancient power, new power, sustaining force
38:4 **LIBERATION & LETTING GO** Freedom comes with unbinding

39:1 **WISDOM** The ability to perceive reality with equanimity
39:2 **EMBODIMENT** The quest for living truth
39:3 **SPIRITUAL PRACTICE** To make room within for the sacred
39:4 **GOODNESS** An echo of the call to come together

40:1 **SIN** Missing the mark, staining the inner life
40:2 **ANGELS & DEMONS** Eternal forms for struggle
40:3 **INTELLIGENCE** Reciprical sharing, human & divine
40:4 **FREE WILL & DESTINY** What is written, and how do
our choices matter?

41:1 **THE DIVINE FEMININE** Creation and the mystery of renewal
41:2 **INNOCENCE & EXPERIENCE** Seeing life anew every moment
41:3 **WAYS OF HEALING** Paths toward wholeness
41:4 **GENEROSITY & SERVICE** To give is divine

42:1 **THE SEARCH FOR MEANING** Why are we alive?
42:2 **HAPPINESS** Finding joy through spiritual work
42:3 **THE SACRED** Touching the Holy in our lives and world
42:4 **FAMILIES** Bonding with others, finding ourselves

43:1 **WEALTH** Sharing earthly and heavenly riches
43:2 **THE MIRACULOUS** The Divine in our midst
43:3 **THE JOURNEY HOME** Returning to the Source
43:4 **HOPE** Finding the light that guides

44:1 **CHANGE AND THE CHANGELESS** Shelter from the storm
44:1 **THE WILD** Celebrating Nature

The Wild
PARABOLA

"In Wildness is the preservation of the World"

Order ONLINE at **WWW.PARABOLA.ORG**

The Return of the Prodigal Son (detail). Rembrandt Harmensz van Rijn, c. 1669. Oil on canvas. The Hermitage, St. Petersburg

The Parable of the Prodigal Son

Pope John Paul II

AT THE VERY BEGINNING of the New Testament, two voices resound in St. Luke's Gospel in unique harmony concerning the mercy of God, a harmony which forcefully echoes the whole Old Testament tradition. They express the semantic elements linked to the differentiated terminology of the ancient books. Mary, entering the house of Zechariah, magnifies the Lord with all her soul for "his mercy," which "from generation to generation" is bestowed on those who fear Him. A little later, as she recalls the election of Israel, she proclaims the mercy which He who has chosen her holds "in remembrance" from all time. Afterwards, in the same house, when John the Baptist is born, his father Zechariah blesses the God of Israel and glorifies Him for performing the mercy promised to our fathers and for remembering His holy covenant.

In the teaching of Christ Himself, this image inherited from the Old Testament becomes at the same time simpler and more profound. This is perhaps most evident in the parable of the prodigal son. Although the word "mercy" does not appear, it nevertheless expresses the essence of the divine mercy in a particularly clear way. This is due not so much to the terminology, as in the Old Testament books, as to the analogy that enables us to understand more fully the very mystery of mercy, as a profound drama played out between the father's love and the prodigality and sin of the son.

That son, who receives from the father the portion of the inheritance that is due to him and leaves home to squander it in a far country "in loose living," in a certain sense is the man of every period, beginning with the one who was the first to lose the inheritance of grace and original justice. The analogy at this point is very wide-ranging. The parable indirectly touches upon every breach of the covenant of love, every loss of grace, every sin. In this analogy there is less emphasis than in the prophetic tradition on the unfaithfulness of the whole people of Israel, although the analogy of the prodigal son may extend to this also. "When he had spent everything," the son "began to be in need," especially as "a great famine arose in that country" to which he had gone after leaving his father's house. And in this situation "he would gladly have fed on" anything, even "the pods that the swine ate," the swine that he herded for "one of the citizens of that country." But even this was refused him.

The analogy turns clearly towards man's interior. The inheritance that the son had received from his father was a quantity of material goods, but more important than these goods was his dignity as a son in his father's house. The situation in which he found himself when he lost the material goods should have made him aware of the loss of that dignity. He had not thought about it previously, when he had asked his father to give him the part of the inheritance that was due to him, in order to go away. He seems not to be conscious of it even now, when he says to himself: "How many of my father's hired servants have bread enough and to spare, but I perish here with hunger." He measures himself by the standard of the goods that he has lost, that he no longer "possesses," while the hired servants of his father's house "possess" them. These words express above all his attitude to material goods; nevertheless under their surface is concealed the tragedy of lost dignity, the awareness of squandered sonship.

It is at this point that he makes the decision: "I will arise and go to my father, and I will say to him, 'Father, I have sinned against heaven and before you; I am no longer worthy to be called your son. Treat me as one of your hired servants.'" These are words that reveal more deeply the essential problem. Through the complex material situation in which the prodigal son found himself because of his folly, because of sin, the sense of lost dignity had matured. When he decides to return to his father's house, to ask his father to be received— no longer by virtue of his right as a son, but as an employee—at first sight he seems to be acting by reason of the hunger and poverty that he had fallen into; this motive, however, is permeated by an awareness of a deeper loss: to be a hired servant in his own father's house is certainly a great humiliation and source of shame. Nevertheless, the prodigal son is ready to undergo that humiliation and shame. He realizes that he no longer has any right except to be an employee in his father's house. His decision is taken in full consciousness of what he has deserved and of what he can still have a right to in accordance with the norms of justice. Precisely this reasoning demonstrates that, at the center of the prodigal son's consciousness, the sense of lost dignity is emerging, the sense of that dignity that springs from the relationship of the son with the father. And it is with this decision that he sets out.

Although the son has squandered the inheritance, nevertheless his humanity is saved. Indeed, it has been, in a way, found again.

In the parable of the prodigal son, the term "justice" is not used even once; just as in the original text the term "mercy" is not used either. Nevertheless, the relationship between justice and love, that is manifested as mercy, is inscribed with great exactness in the content of the Gospel parable. It becomes more evident that love is transformed into mercy when it is necessary to go beyond the precise norm of justice—precise and often too narrow. The prodigal son, having wasted the property he received from his father, deserves—after his return—to earn his living by working in his father's house as a hired servant and possibly, little by little, to build up a certain provision of material goods, though perhaps never as much as the amount he had squandered. This would be demanded by the order of justice, especially as the son had not only squandered the part of the inheritance belonging to him but had also hurt and offended his father by his whole conduct. Since this conduct had in his own eyes deprived him of his dignity as a son, it could not be a matter of indifference to his father. It was bound to make him suffer. It was also bound to implicate him in some way. And yet, after all, it was his own son who was involved, and such a relationship could never be altered or destroyed by any sort of behavior. The prodigal son is aware of this and it is precisely this awareness that shows him clearly the dignity which he has lost and which makes him honestly evaluate the position that he could still expect in his father's house.

This exact picture of the prodigal son's state of mind enables us to understand exactly what the mercy of God consists in. There is no doubt that in this simple but penetrating analogy the figure of the father reveals to us God as Father. The conduct of the father in the parable and his whole behavior, which manifests his internal attitude, enables us to rediscover the individual threads of the Old Testament vision of mercy in a synthesis which is totally new, full of simplicity and depth. The father of the prodigal son is faithful to his fatherhood, faithful to the love that he had always lavished on his son. This fidelity is expressed in the parable not only by his immediate readiness to welcome him home when he returns after having squandered his inheritance; it is expressed even more fully by that joy, that merrymaking for the squanderer after his return, merrymaking which is so generous that it provokes the opposition and hatred of the elder brother, who had never gone far away from his father and had never abandoned the home.

The father's fidelity to himself—a trait already known by the Old Testament term *hesed*—is at the same time expressed in a manner particularly charged with affection. We read, in fact, that when the father saw the prodigal son returning home "he had compassion, ran to meet him, threw his arms around his neck and kissed him." He certainly does this under the influence of a deep affection, and this also explains his generosity towards his son, that generosity which so angers the elder son. Nevertheless, the causes of this emotion are to be sought at a deeper level. Notice, the father is aware that a fundamental good has been saved: the good of his son's humanity. Although the son has squandered the inheritance, nevertheless his humanity is saved. Indeed, it has been, in a way, found again. The father's words to the elder son reveal this: "It was fitting to make merry and be glad, for this your brother was dead and is alive; he was lost and is found." In the same chapter fifteen of Luke's Gospel, we read the parable of the sheep that was found and then the parable of the coin that was found. Each time there is an emphasis on the same joy that is present in the case of the prodigal son. The father's fidelity to himself is totally concentrated upon the humanity of the lost son, upon his dignity. This explains above all his joyous emotion at the moment of the son's return home.

Going on, one can therefore say that the love for the son, the love that springs from the very essence of fatherhood, in a way obliges the father to be concerned about his son's dignity. This concern is the measure of his love, the love of which Saint Paul was to write: "Love is patient and kind... love does not insist on its own way; it is not irritable or resentful...but rejoices in the right...hopes all things, endures all things" and "love never ends." Mercy—as Christ has presented it in the parable of the prodigal son—has the interior form of the love that in the New Testament is called agape. This love is able to reach down to every prodigal son, to every human misery, and above all to every form of moral misery, to sin. When this happens, the person who is the object of mercy does not feel humiliated, but rather found again and "restored to value." The father first and foremost expresses to him his joy that he has been "found again" and that he has "returned to life. This joy indicates a good that has remained intact: even if he is a prodigal, a son does not cease to be truly his father's son; it also indicates a good that has been found again, which in the case of the prodigal son was his return to the truth about himself.

What took place in the relationship between the father and the son in Christ's parable is not to be evaluated "from the outside." Our prejudices about mercy are mostly the result of appraising them only from the outside. At times it happens that by following this method of evaluation we see in mercy above all a relationship of inequality between the one offering it and the one receiving it. And, in consequence, we are quick to deduce that mercy belittles the receiver, that it offends the dignity of man. The parable of the prodigal son shows that the reality is different: the relationship of mercy is based on the common experience of that good which is man, on the common experience of the dignity that is proper to him. This common experience makes the prodigal son begin to see himself and his actions in their full truth (this vision in truth is a genuine form of humility); on the other hand, for this very reason he becomes a particular good for his father: the father sees so clearly the good which has been achieved thanks to a mysterious radiation of truth and love, that he seems to forget all the evil which the son had committed.

The parable of the prodigal son expresses in a simple but profound way the reality of conversion. Conversion is the most concrete expression of the working of love and of the presence of mercy in the human world. The true and proper meaning of mercy does not consist only in looking, however penetratingly and compassionately, at moral, physical or material evil: mercy is manifested in its true and proper aspect when it restores to value, promotes and draws good from all the forms of evil existing in the world and in man. Understood in this way, mercy constitutes the fundamental content of the messianic message of Christ and the constitutive power of His mission.

His disciples and followers understood and practiced mercy in the same way. Mercy never ceased to reveal itself, in their hearts and in their actions, as an especially creative proof of the love which does not allow itself to be "conquered by evil," but overcomes "evil with good." The genuine face of mercy has to be ever revealed anew. In spite of many prejudices, mercy seems particularly necessary for our times. ◆

Excerpted from Pope John Paul II's 1980 encyclical, "*Dives in Misericordia* (Rich in Mercy)": http://w2.vatican.va/content/john-paul-ii/en/encyclicals/documents/hf_jp-ii_enc_30111980_dives-in-misericordia.html

The Return of the Prodigal Son (detail). Rembrandt Harmensz van Rijn, c. 1669. Oil on canvas. The Hermitage, St. Petersburg

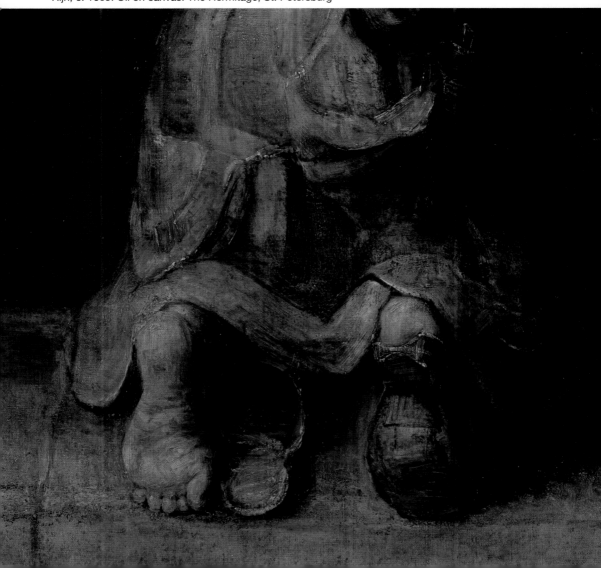

The Parable of the Prodigal Son

THEN [JESUS] SAID: "A certain man had two sons. And the younger of them said to *his* father, 'Father, give me the portion of goods that falls *to me.*' So he divided to them *his* livelihood. And not many days after, the younger son gathered all together, journeyed to a far country, and there wasted his possessions with prodigal living. But when he had spent all, there arose a severe famine in that land, and he began to be in want. Then he went and joined himself to a citizen of that country, and he sent him into his fields to feed swine. And he would gladly have filled his stomach with the pods that the swine ate, and no one gave him *anything.*

"But when he came to himself, he said, 'How many of my father's hired servants have bread enough and to spare, and I perish with hunger! I will arise and go to my father, and will say to him, 'Father, I have sinned against heaven and before you, and I am no longer worthy to be called your son. Make me like one of your hired servants.'"

"And he arose and came to his father. But when he was still a great way off, his father saw him and had compassion, and ran and fell on his neck and kissed him. And the son said to him, 'Father, I have sinned against heaven and in your sight, and am no longer worthy to be called your son.'

"But the father said to his servants, 'Bring out the best robe and put *it* on him, and put a ring on *his* hand and sandals on *his* feet. And bring the fatted calf here and kill *it*, and let us eat and be merry; for this my son was dead and is alive again; he was lost and is found.' And they began to be merry.

"Now his older son was in the field. And as he came and drew near to the house, he heard music and dancing. So he called one of the servants and asked what these things meant. And he said to him, 'Your brother has come, and because he has received him safe and sound, your father has killed the fatted calf.'

"But he was angry and would not go in. Therefore his father came out and pleaded with him. So he answered and said to *his* father, 'Lo, these many years I have been serving you; I never transgressed your commandment at any time; and yet you never gave me a young goat, that I might make merry with my friends. But as soon as this son of yours came, who has devoured your livelihood with harlots, you killed the fatted calf for him.'

"And he said to him, 'Son, you are always with me, and all that I have is yours. It was right that we should make merry and be glad, for your brother was dead and is alive again, and was lost and is found.'" ◆

Luke 15: 11–32, New King James Version

Book Review

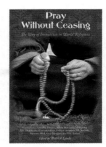

PRAY WITHOUT CEASING:
The Way of the Invocation in World Religions

EDITED BY PATRICK LAUDE. WORLD WISDOM (WWW.WORLDWISDOM.COM).
2006. PP. 240. $19.95 PAPER

Reviewed by Samuel Bendeck Sotillos

"Pray without ceasing." (I Thessalonians 5:17)

IF THE PRESUPPOSITION held is that the human being exists in both the horizontal and vertical domains, that is both in time and what is timeless, both in the physical and that of the metaphysical, it is easier to comprehend and consequently situate the significance of prayer as a quintessential bridge between these two distinct domains. Without prayer as a vital link to connect these two domains, they remain separate, opaque, and disconnected, as if impervious to one another without the aid of a higher reality. It can be argued that without prayer, it is not possible to be truly what the human state is intended to be in its most complete sense. Yet to think and see from this point of view in an era so deprived of the sacred one needs to be vigilant about the very presuppositions held about the nature of reality and the course this paves for the wayfarer on the Path. We cannot overlook that the modern world and its prolongation the postmodern world are not neutral or value-free—that is, without their own theoretical tenets that are antagonistic to metaphysics and integral spirituality.

Jung's legendary American lectures on dream interpretation

Dream Symbols of the Individuation Process
Notes of C. G. Jung's Seminars on Wolfgang Pauli's Dreams
C. G. Jung, edited by Suzanne Gieser
Cloth $39.95
Philemon Foundation Series

PRINCETON UNIVERSITY PRESS

This anthology compiled by Patrick Laude (*SHIMMERING MIRRORS*; *PATHWAYS TO AN INNER ISLAM*, etc.) provides extraordinary foundational texts on the experience of prayer that are complemented by essays on the remembrance and realization of the Divine. According to diverse saints and sages, to abide in the Divine Name is to abide in none other than the Divine Presence itself, meaning there is no distinction between the Name and the Named. The Name is none other than the transpersonal reality itself. Prayer allows for a direct relationship with the Divine, establishing a link between the human and the Divine. When surveying the diverse traditions and the mystical dimensions of the world's religions, it becomes apparent that prayer defines the centrality of the human condition and holds an eschatological relevance. This is because human beings cannot

go beyond themselves by effort alone; they need an agency that transcends the empirical ego. Prayer provides an integral method of accessing the transpersonal dimension known as *japa-yoga* in Hinduism, *nembutsu* in Buddhism, Jesus Prayer in Christianity, and *dhikr* in Islam. In his insightful introduction to the book, Laude explains that "the invocation is not only a prayer of the human to the Divine, it is also a prayer of the Divine to itself through a human intermediary." He adds, "The invocation realizes the *raison d'être* of all religious practices since the latter ultimately aim at recognizing, remembering, and assimilating the supreme Reality." It has also been underscored that in order to make this pilgrimage to the One, spiritual guidance and an affiliation to a divine Revelation is needed for the methodic repetition or invocation of the Divine Name to be efficacious.

It is imperative to define our terms and recall that the etymological root of the English word "religion" is from the Latin *religare*, meaning to "to re-bind" or "to bind back" by implication to the Divine or a transcendent Reality. The function of prayer is to do just this, to assist in the reintegration of the human with the Divine. In fact, each of the world's religions provides doctrines (theories) and methods (practices) on how to make the journey or return to the Spirit. Prayer from this perspective informs in its wholeness what human identity is *in divinis*.

Within the Hindu tradition (known as the *sanātana dharma* or "eternal religion"), the medieval poet and philosopher Tulsīdās, frames the paramount nature that prayer holds in

the final phase of the temporal cycle and its essential connection to the invocation of the Divine Name: "In this *Kali* Age salvation is not gained by knowledge, karma, and worship. But only by taking shelter in the Name." Śrī Rāmakrishna makes a providential observation concerning the Divine Name and its identification with the transpersonal dimension: "God and His name are identical". Swami Ramdas confirms this same teaching, "God and His Name are not distinct from one another. The Name is God Himself." According to the *Bhagavad Gītā* it is sufficient at the moment of death to recall the Divine Name in order to abide in the divine Presence itself:

> And at the hour of death, he who dies
> Remembering Me,
> Having relinquished the body,

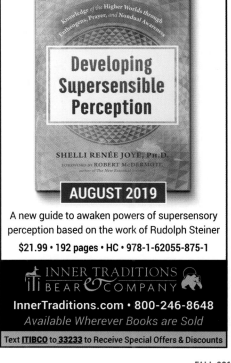

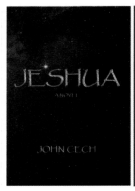
Goes to My state of being.
In this matter there is no doubt....

It is furthermore added,

Therefore, at all times
Meditate on Me (or: Remember Me
[*mam anusmara*])
With your mind and intellect
Fixed on Me.
In this way, you shall surely come
To Me....

Chaitanya, who revitalized the *bhakti* movement in India, emphasizes that the practice of the invocation of the Divine Name can be observed in all situations and at all moments of the day and is available to all seekers regardless of one's ethnic, racial, socio-economic, or religious identity:

The names of the Lord are many, they are filled with power like Himself and He has laid down no laws regarding their repetition. (They can be repeated anywhere and at all times by anybody of any caste, age, or denomination.) Alas! such is His Grace, and yet we on our part have not yet developed full love and enthusiasm for the name of the Lord.

Swami Ramdas tirelessly emphasized the universality of this spiritual practice that is available to all, "whatever race, caste, creed, or color you may belong, take up the Name of God."

A renowned exponent of *Advaita Vedānta* or non-duality, Shankara recognizes the spiritual validity of *japa* when writing: "Remember, nothing

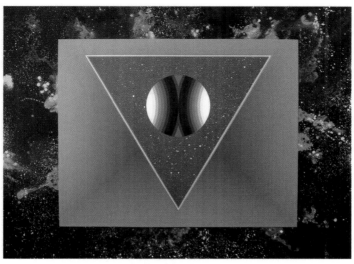

Yoni and the Universe

can save thee at the last moment except the shelter of the Lord, so sing thou His sweet Name Govinda! Govinda!.... Indulge not in formal ceremonies. Dwell in the Atman. Cross the Ocean of transmigration singing the sweet name—Govinda! Govinda! Govinda!" Shankara elsewhere writes, "Control thy soul, restrain thy breathing, distinguish the transitory from the True, repeat the holy Name of God, and thus calm the agitated mind. To this universal rule apply thyself with all thy heart and all thy soul." When a devotee asked Ramana Maharshi the following question: "Can *advaita* be realized by *japa* of holy names; say Rāma, Krishna, etc.?" The Sage of Arunachala unequivocally affirmed, "Yes."

Kabīr, who was regarded as a saint by Hindus, Sikhs, and Muslims alike, stressed that: "The True Name is the

only thing to repeat. It is the best gift to make." The highly esteemed bhakti poet Mīrābāī recalls discovering the Divine Name and its impact on her life: "I discovered the great secret in uttering the Name and adhering to this quintessence of *sāstras* (scriptures), I reached my Girdhar through prayers and tears."

Within the Buddhist tradition, Hōnen stresses the practice of *nembutsu* or the invocation of the name of Amida: "cease from all other religious practices, apply yourself to the Nembutsu alone." He recounts the Buddha Shakyamuni, expressing, "Give yourself with undivided mind to the repetition of the name of the Buddha who is in Himself endless life." The chief disciple of Hōnen, Shinran, makes an important link between the invocation of the Divine Name and mindfulness practice: "Saying the Name is constant mindfulness." Respected author on Tibetan Buddhism Marco Pallis points out that the six-syllabled formula *Om mani padme Hum*, while facilitating complex mystical correspondences, contains "the quintessence of the teaching of all the Buddhas."

Within the Jewish tradition, the Old Testament instructs: "I will praise Thy Name continuously and will extol it in all things." (Ecclesiastes 51) Rabbi Isaac of Akko discusses the mystery of the Divine Name and its connection between the finite and the Infinite as a means of transpersonal union within the Jewish tradition and its mystical dimension:

> Remember God and God's love constantly. Let your thought not be separated from God. I declare, both to individuals and to the masses: If you want to know the secret of binding your soul above and joining your thought to God— so that by means of such continuous contemplation you attain incessantly the world that is coming, and so that God be with you always, in this life and the next— then place in front of the eyes of your mind the letters of God's name, as if they were written in a book in Hebrew script. Visualize every letter extending to infinity. What I mean is: when you visualize the letters, focus on them with your mind's eye as you contemplate infinity. Both together: gazing and meditating.

Maimonides explains that only those who received special instruction were permitted to invoke the tetragrammation YHVH:

> A priestly blessing has been prescribed for us, in which the name of the Eternal (YHVH) is pronounced as it is written

(and not in the form of a substituted name) and that name is the "explicit name." It was not generally known how the name had to be pronounced, nor how it was proper to vocalize the separate letters, nor whether any of the letters which could be doubled should in fact be doubled. Men who had received special instruction transmitted this one to another (that is, the manner of pronouncing this name) and taught it to none but their chosen disciples....

Within the Christian tradition, we recall the words: "Whosoever shall call on the name of the Lord shall be saved" (Acts 2:21). Saint Philotheos of Sinai discloses that remembrance itself is to be in the divine Presence: "The blessed remembrance of God—which is the very presence of Jesus." In the classic of Eastern Orthodox spirituality THE WAY OF A PILGRIM, an anonymous seeker receives a powerful and memorable instruction

from his spiritual father on how to practice the Jesus Prayer or the Prayer of the Heart:

> The continuous interior Prayer of Jesus is a constant uninterrupted calling upon the divine Name of Jesus with the lips, in the spirit, in the heart; while forming a mental picture of His constant presence, and imploring His grace, during every occupation, at all times, in all places, even during sleep. The appeal is couched in these terms, "Lord Jesus Christ, have mercy on me." One who accustoms himself to this appeal experiences as a result so deep a consolation and so great a need to offer the prayer always, that he can no longer live without it, and it will continue to voice itself within him of its own accord.

The Islamic tradition highlights the paramount nature of remembrance as instructed in the Qur'ān: "Remember Me, and I shall remember you" (2:152), "Your Lord hath said: Call upon Me and I will answer you" (40:60), and "To God belong the most beautiful Names, so call upon Him by them" (7:180). Within the mystical dimension of Islam, also known as tasawwuf or Sufism, Ibn 'Atā' Allāh Al-Iskandarī asserts, "Invoking causes God's remembrance of the servant, which is the greatest honor and loftiest distinction." He continues, "Invoking removes hardness from the heart and engenders tenderness and mildness. Forgetfulness of the heart is a disease and an ailment, while remembrance is a cure for the invoker from every malady and symptom." From a spiritual point of view, life and death take on a different meaning as indicated in the following: "The invoker is alive even if he be dead; while the forgetful man, even though he is alive, is actually to be counted among the dead." Shaykh Ahmad Al-'Alawī also emphasized the importance of the way of invocation as a means of fixing consciousness on the divine Reality: "Remembrance is the mightiest rule of the religion....The law was not enjoined upon us, neither were the rites of worship ordained, but for the sake of establishing the remembrance of God." He also stressed that this remembrance "is not to be restricted to a certain time or place, but can be practiced at all times and in all places." Rūmī poetically speaks to the role of invocation of the Divine Name: "Do not apply musk to the body, rub it on the heart. / What is musk? The sacred name of Him who is full of Majesty."

Within the Shamanic or primordial religion of the First Peoples, as Patrick Laude points out:

In shamanistic practices the world over, as in Africa or in Central Asia, invocations are numerous, pervading the whole of life: every qualitative action, in craft for instance, is introduced by a specific invocation that effects an "actualization" of the invisible entities, or an "animation" of the "matter" of the activity. This animation by the word is expressed by a sense of the "power" (*nyame*) inherent in invocations....[T]he shamanistic path primarily invokes an increased receptivity to the presence of the Divine in Nature. In that sense pure receptivity is in itself a kind of invocation.

Medicine man and Sun Dance Chief Thomas Yellowtail states the following about the practice of the invocation of the Divine Name: "Each day, whatever I am doing, I am always praying and thinking of God...all the time I am

praying…continually praying to God, remembering the name of God."

It has been shown that spiritual aspirants are unable to directly contemplate the transpersonal domain. They therefore require symbols in order to access the transcendent, as Titus Burckhardt eloquently illustrates: "Man cannot concentrate directly on the Infinite, but, by concentrating on the symbol of the Infinite, attains to the Infinite Itself." Frithjof Schuon summarizes the significance of the invocation of the Divine Name and its relationship to the Absolute:

> The sufficient reason for the invocation of the Name is the "remembering of God"; in the final analysis this is nothing other than consciousness of the Absolute. The Name actualizes this consciousness and, in the end, perpetuates it in the soul and

fixes it in the heart, so that it penetrates the whole being and at the same time transmutes and absorbs it. Consciousness of the Absolute is the prerogative of human intelligence and also its aim.

French philosopher Simone Weil also affirms the way of invocation as it applies across the diverse religions: "Every religious practice, every rite, all liturgy is a form of the recitation of the name of the Lord". Leo Schaya articulates the important function of the invocation of the Divine Name: "God, by invoking his creative and redemptive name, causes everything that exists to issue from him and to return into him; by invoking his name with him, every being is born from him, lives by him, and is united with him."

The editor of this volume deserves to be congratulated for this timely

work, which is a true gem in that it not only highlights unique and diverse religious and mystical perspectives, but elucidates on their central spiritual method of prayer and the invocation of the Divine Name as it is found across all of the world's sapiential traditions. It is this practice of remembrance that facilitates the human being's journey or rather return to the Absolute. In a single volume one will find powerful illustrations of this central practice, which would require significant effort and time to compile from diverse sources. This is an excellent reference book that will provide tremendous value for seekers and students of comparative religion, esoterism, or mysticism, interfaith dialogue, and cross-cultural studies as it demonstrates the common ground on which the transcendent unity of religions may be realized. Through the way of remembrance, the human

being can realize the divine Unity that is both immanent and transcendent and that is a reflection of integral human identity *in divinis*. Many are the paths and ways to the One, yet through the universal spiritual practice of the invocation of the Divine Name this reality can be crystallized in the heart and mind of the wayfarer so that, as Antony the Great explains, there is no one praying, only the actualization of prayer itself: "The only real prayer is the one in which we are no longer aware that we are praying." ◆

Samuel Bendeck Sotillos is a practicing psychotherapist. His focus of interest is comparative religion and the interface between spirituality and psychology. His works include Behaviorism: The Quandary of a Psychology with a Soul and Psychology, Without Spirit: The Freudian Quandary, *and he is the editor of* Psychology and the Perennial Philosophy. *His writing has appeared in* Sacred Web, Sophia, **Parabola**, Resurgence, Temenos Academy Review, *and* Studies in Comparative Religion.

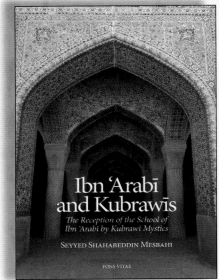

October 23rd - 27th 2019, San José, CA

SAND

FROM QUARKS TO LOVE

conversations / workshops / dance
experiential sessions / art / community

Join us for a 5-day immersive experience where
leading scientists, philosophers, spiritual teachers and you
will gather to explore a new understanding of
who we really are, both as individuals and as a society.

deborah
JOHNSON

david
EAGLEMAN

lama
TSOMO

thomas
HUEBL

ADYASHANTI

rupert
SPIRA

sará
KING

james
DOTY

jean
HOUSTON

mirabai
STARR

WWW.SCIENCEANDNONDUALITY.COM

🕉=mc²
SCIENCE & NONDUALITY
CONFERENCE

PARABOLA *needs your help!*

Parabola brings timeless wisdom to troubled times. As a longtime reader of the magazine recently wrote, "I continue to appreciate Parabola as the most compelling and thoughtful spiritual publication out there. It is filling a vast need in a wounded but still beautiful world."

Now we urgently need your help to carry on. *Parabola* is a nonprofit, independent, reader-supported publication. In order to publish each issue, we depend directly upon the generosity of readers like you. Without your support, there would be no *Parabola*.

Please help us to bring Parabola's treasures to the world. Along with future issues on the themes of The Goddess, Quest, and Presence, in coming months we will continue to digitize our vast archives, reviving decades of insight and beauty.

Will you please help us by making a meaningful and tax-deductible donation? You can donate online at www.parabola.org, or by mailing a check to Parabola, 20 West 20th Street, 2nd Floor, New York, NY 10011. Please feel free to get in touch with me to discuss your donation, or to plan for monthly or estate giving, at jeffzaleski1@gmail.com or by telephone at 212-822-8806.

A contribution of any size will be greatly appreciated! To those of you who can donate $50 or more, we are happy to offer in return:

- $50 or higher donation: One free gift subscription
- $100 or higher donation: Two free gift subscriptions
- $250 or higher donation: Three free gift subscriptions
- $500 or higher: Three free gift subscriptions and a *Parabola* tote bag
- $1000 or higher: Three free subscriptions; a *Parabola* tote bag; lunch with *Parabola* editors

Thank you for your support.

Jeff Zaleski
Editor and Publisher, *Parabola*

CREDITS

PROFILES

PAULA ARAI is the Urmila Gopal Singhal Professor in the Religions of India at Louisiana State University. She is the author of *BRINGING ZEN HOME* and *WOMEN LIVING ZEN*.

SEANE CORN is an internationally renowned yoga teacher. She is the cofounder of Off The Mat, Into The World®, a global humanitarian leadership training program. She teaches extensively at workshops, conferences, and retreats throughout the U.S. and abroad. For more information, please visit seanecorn.com and offthematintotheworld.org.

BETSY CORNWELL is *Parabola*'s Story Editor. She is the author of the novels *TIDES*, *MECHANICA*, *VENTURESS*, and *THE FOREST QUEEN*.

RABBI TIRZAH FIRESTONE is an author, a Jungian psychotherapist, and founding rabbi of Congregation Nevei Kodesh in Boulder, Colorado.

GESSHIN CLAIRE GREENWOOD is the author of *JUST ENOUGH AND BOW FIRST, ASK QUESTIONS LATER*, and writes the blog *THATSOZEN*. Ordained as a Buddhist nun in Japan by Seido Suzuki Roshi in 2010, she received her dharma transmission in 2015. Please visit Gesshin.net for more information.

ALEXANDRA HAVEN is *Parabola*'s Managing Editor and a library assistant for the Bodleian Libraries.

KENT JONES is a filmmaker, writer, and director of the New York Film Festival. He is the author of *PHYSICAL EVIDENCE: SELECTED FILM CRITICISM*. His films include *VAL LEWTON: THE MAN IN THE SHADOWS, HITCHCOCK/TRUFFAUT*, and, most recently, *DIANE*.

SATISH KUMAR is a long-time peace and environment activist, and is a former Jain monk. Editor of *RESURGENCE* magazine from 1973-2016, he founded Devon's Schumacher College and is the author of several books, including *ELEGANT SIMPLICITY: THE ART OF LIVING WELL*.

KENNETH E. LAWRENCE is a writer and musician. He and his wife, artist KUMIKO LAWRENCE, are Soju Projekt (www.sojukai.com), a performance group focusing on tales from legends and epics of the world.

ELEANOR O'HANLON is a writer and conservationist who has worked as a field researcher for leading international conservation groups. Her book

EYES OF THE WILD (eyesofthewild.org) won the 2015 Nautilus Gold Book Award for Nature.

POPE JOHN PAUL II (1920-2005), born Karol Józef Wojtyła, served as head of the Roman Catholic Church from 1978 until his death.

ELIZABETH RANDALL is a high-school English teacher and author. Her books include *THE FLOATING TEACHER* and *HAUNTED ST. AUGUSTINE AND ST. JOHNS COUNTY*.

MARTIN SCORSESE is an Academy Award-winning filmmaker and historian. Among his many films are *TAXI DRIVER, RAGING BULL, CASINO, THE DEPARTED, SILENCE*, and *THE IRISHMAN*.

RICHARD SMOLEY is a consulting editor to *Parabola* and editor of *QUEST: JOURNAL OF THE THEOSOPHICAL SOCIETY IN AMERICA*. His latest book, *A THEOLOGY OF LOVE: REIMAGINING CHRISTIANITY THROUGH "A COURSE IN MIRACLES,"* is due to be published in November 2019.

MIRABAI STARR is an international speaker and teacher of the mystics, contemplative practice, and the transformational power of grief and loss. She is the author of *GOD OF LOVE, CARAVAN OF NO DESPAIR*, and *WILD MERCY: LIVING THE FIERCE AND TENDER WISDOM OF THE WOMEN MYSTICS*. For more information, please visit mirabaistarr.com.

IWASAKI TSUNEO (1917-2002) was a Japanese biologist and artist who created a strikingly original body of modern Buddhist artwork, ranging from classical Buddhist iconography to majestic views of our universe as revealed by science, created with the use miniature calligraphies of the Heart Sutra.

DESMOND TUTU is a South African Anglican cleric and theologian best known as an anti-apartheid and human rights activist. He was awarded the Nobel Peace Prize in 1984.

LEE VAN LAER is a Senior Editor of *Parabola*. For more information, please visit www.doremishock.com.

LLEWELLYN VAUGHAN-LEE is a Sufi teacher in the Naqshbandiyya-Mujaddidiyya Sufi Order. He is the founder of The Golden Sufi Center and is the author of several books, most recently *INCLUDING THE EARTH IN OUR PRAYERS: A GLOBAL DIMENSION TO SPIRITUAL PRACTICE*.

Endpoint

Caritas. Pieter Bruegel the Elder, 1559. Drawing, pen in brown ink. Museum Boijmans Van Beuningen, Rotterdam, The Netherlands. Counterclockwise from lower right are the Works of Mercy: feed the hungry, give drink to the thirsty, ransom the captive, bury the dead, shelter the stranger, comfort the sick, clothe the naked.

IN THE GOSPEL ACCORDING TO MATTHEW, chapter 25, Jesus says that "when the Son of Man comes in his glory," he will separate humanity "as a shepherd separates the sheep from the goats." And he will say to the sheep, "Come, blessed of my Father, inherit the Kingdom prepared for you from the foundation of the world; for I was hungry, and you gave me food to eat. I was thirsty, and you gave me drink. I was a stranger, and you took me in. I was naked, and you clothed me. I was sick, and you visited me. I was in prison, and you came to me."

From this statement, the Catholic Church derives the first six of its Corporal Works of Mercy (the seventh, "to bury the dead," comes from the Book of Tobit.) These works are complemented by seven Spiritual Works of Mercy, which include: to instruct the ignorant; to counsel the doubtful; to admonish the sinners; to bear patiently those who wrong us; to forgive offenses; to comfort the afflicted; and to pray for the living and the dead.

Notably, in 2016 Pope Francis suggested a new work of mercy: Care for creation, with both corporeal and spiritual components. Corporally, because it promotes "daily gestures which break with the logic of violence, exploitation and selfishness"; spiritually, as it promotes contemplation of creation to discern what God is teaching us through it. ◆